MUSIC IN TEXAS

AMS PRESS

NEW YORK

MUSIC IN TEXAS

A SURVEY OF ONE ASPECT OF

CULTURAL PROGRESS

LOTA M. SPELL

Austin, Texas

1936

Library of Congress Cataloging in Publication Data

Spell, Lota May (Harrigan) 1885–
    Music in Texas.

    Reprint of the 1936 ed., Austin Texas.
    1. Music--Texas--History and criticism.
I. Title.
ML200.7.T4S6   1973   780'.9764   72-1675
ISBN 0-404-09907-6

Trim size of original edition: 5 5/8 X 8 7/8
Trim size of AMS edition: 5 1/2 X 8 1/2

Reprinted from an original copy in the collections of
the University of Pennsylvania Library

From the edition of 1936, Austin
First AMS edition published in 1973
Manufactured in the United States of America

AMS PRESS INC.
NEW YORK, N.Y. 10003

PREFACE

THE purpose of this work is to make available to teachers, club workers, and others interested in the cultural development of the State of Texas some facts by which the progress of music may be traced, and also some songs actually sung through the years, as illustrative material. Many of these, here reproduced from early editions in the possession of the writer, while in no sense masterpieces of musical art, are representative of the taste of the people at different eras. A collection of dances and instrumental music will be issued separately in larger format later.

The thanks of the writer for assistance are due to too many to call each by name. Especial thanks are due Dr. R. C. Stephenson for the translation of the Spanish songs; and to Dr. Eduard Micek, Dr. Carlos Castañeda, Miss Hilda Widen and Miss Julia Harris, of Austin; Miss Julia Owen of Navasota; Sr. Julio Galindo of Mexico City; Miss Jovita Gonzáles and Mr. Oscar Fox of San Antonio; Mrs. Selma Metzenthin-Raunick and Mr. H. M. Dietel of New Braunfels; and Dr. Charles B. Qualia of Lubbock, for aid in locating materials. Without the interest and insistence of the officers and members of the State Federation of Music Clubs the work would never have been completed or issued.

The courtesy of Silver, Burdett and Company in permitting the use of "Clang, Clang," "Choosing a Flower," and "At the Window" from the *Progressive Music Series;* of Oscar Fox and Whitney Montgomery for "Corn Silks and Cotton Blossoms"; of the Adolf Fuchs Memorial Association for the use of the Fuchs songs; and of Dr. H. F. Estill for his adaptation of the text of "Will you come to the Bower" is gratefully acknowledged.

To my aunt,
Lota Dashiell,
born in Texas, 1853,
who sang to me, in my childhood,
the songs of early Texas;
and to the members of the
State Federation of Music Clubs,
whose insistence led to its preparation;
this work is dedicated

TABLE OF CONTENTS

Book I. The Period of Dissemination

Book II. Absorption from a Wider Field

Book III. The Period of Amalgamation

Book IV. The Beginnings of Creative Work

LIST OF SONGS INCLUDED

LIST OF ILLUSTRATIONS

BOOK I

The Period of Dissemination

CHAPTER I

Music Among the Indians

FOUR hundred years ago the great stretch of land between the Rio Grande and Red River was inhabited only by wandering Indians engaged largely in hunting, fishing, and fighting any other tribes who trespassed upon their hunting grounds. All were of a low degree of civilization, if by that term we understand the practice of having fixed homes, knowledge of the useful arts such as tool-making, home building, stock raising, crop growing, spinning and weaving, and mastery of means of transmitting experience to those who lived after them. The Indians who roamed the wilds of Texas even two centuries ago were still nomadic, some were even cannibalistic. It is easy to understand that among a people who lived only to eat and fight such a thing as culture was long unknown. For culture, and music is one form of it, can come into existence only after the barest necessities of life have been met. Until a man can protect himself against the weather and his enemies, and discover ways of securing food, he will not likely turn his attention to drawing pictures, modeling, making music, or writing books. And that is the reason that music and other forms of culture—the finer elements in a man's life— were very slow in developing in Texas.

Nevertheless the earliest music in Texas was that of the Indians. On first thought it seems surprising that an Indian, who lived almost entirely in the open and gathered his food day by day, moving about whenever the game supply became scarce, and who had little care for the future, should ever know anything about music. But people who live in the great outdoors hear the music of Nature, which the child of the city seldom hears. The Indian heard the sounds of the water, of the leaves on the trees, of the birds in the woods, and many other sounds only heard in the country. And he must have tried to imitate some of the sounds he heard. So long as he used his voice only in talking, his range of pitch was small; but when he began to imitate the songs of the winds and the birds, he raised and lowered his voice and used new tones he had never needed before. And when he did so, he had begun to create one element of music—melody.

All peoples who have spent their lives largely in the open have noticed the marvellous things happening about them, and long ago they discovered that many seem to follow a regular routine. They observed the regularity with which the sun and moon rose and set, the paths the stars travelled, the rise and fall of the tides, the coming of spring and winter, the beginning and the end of plant, animal, and human life. They became aware that within themselves the heart beat by a regular pattern; the lungs breathed in and out; in order even to walk or run, the feet are raised and put down again regularly. And from all those things, primitive people like the Indians gained some feeling for what we call rhythm--the repetition of some certain pattern. They noticed that in order to have rhythm some contrast was always necessary—the heart beat loud and soft; the lungs breathed in and out; the sun rose and set, as did the moon and stars; the tides rose and fell; in each and every pattern there was the contrast of strong and weak, of loud and soft, of an accent and the lack of it. When they began to imitate any of these patterns they made accented and unaccented sounds by striking with sticks or stones on hollow logs, thereby creating rhythm; after a while they found they could make better sounds by striking on skins stretched across the ends of hollow logs; then they had begun to construct musical instruments, drums. When they began to beat on logs or drums as an accompaniment to the tread of their feet on the ground, they were composing march rhythms. Soon they were clapping their hands or moving different parts of their bodies according to some regular pattern; then they were dancing. When they imitated the beat of their hearts, they used double rhythm; from the action of their lungs, they learned to create triple rhythms. And, even so long ago, they realized that when they sang or danced no faster than their hearts beat normally, the music was quiet and satisfying and made them feel contented; when they sang or danced faster, their blood was stirred to quicker action and they were soon ready to fight.

It has always been true that when people notice the marvelous things that happen about them, they soon begin to wonder what great power directs everything. From that wonder came religion—a feeling of awe and respect for some power greater than man can understand. To that mysterious being who sent the rain and the storm, the Texas Indian early directed his prayers; in honor of that Invisible Spirit he danced and sang as best he could. So music came into use as an aid in appealing to the Great Power above. By moving parts of his body, by beating on wood or stones, by blowing through reeds or shell horns, and by raising his voice to a greater range than in speaking—which is usually only five tones—he tried to imitate some of the sounds he heard, and this gave him intense pleasure. As he thought that what gave him pleasure would also please his Great Father, he danced and sang with great fervor in his prayers and ceremonies. With the Indian began the association in Texas of music and religion.

The Texas Indian made other uses of music. The squaw crooned tunes to her baby, who made his first attempts at producing rhythms on a rattle made from a gourd filled with tiny stones. When the young brave went courting, he sang or played tunes on a reed to lure the maiden he loved from her wigwam. When one of the tribe was sick, the Medicine Man called in some of the best singers, or himself sang over the sick one in order to drive away the evil spirits. When the brave went to war, he made noises on his drum or with his rattles or shell horns, to arouse all to action. Such music seemed to stir them to increased effort.

Although he learned from his great teacher, Nature, something of those essential elements of music—melody and rhythm—the Texas Indian never learned any way of writing down his music so that others might play and sing just what he did. His music was taught by sheer imitation—the young Indian did what he heard his elders do. This is the reason that none of the songs the early Indians sang has been preserved in its original form. From the accounts of white men who visited them later we know that they had various types of songs; many were wild and blood-curdling; others were like a quiet chant. To these white men, who knew so much more about music, that of the Indians sounded like a lot of noise such as children make with rattles, sticks of wood, and crude drums; it did not seem worth preserving. But today we wish we knew just what the Indian sang in Texas before the white man came, and what the rhythms were he beat on his crude drum.

(5)

CHAPTER II

Music in the Texas Mission

ABOUT a quarter of a century after Columbus discovered America, some of the Spaniards cruising about the Gulf of Mexico landed on the coast. Led by propitious Fates, they climbed an ever-ascending road westward until from a great height they saw nestling in a tropical valley a city which they soon learned was the capital of the Aztecs, a highly civilized Indian tribe. By a series of fortunate circumstances, the small band of foreigners quickly made themselves the masters of what is today called Mexico City. By 1521, the leader, Hernán Cortez, was begging that missionaries be sent from Spain to convert these Indians to Christianity and to assist in the conquest of other regions. The first three came in 1523; and thereafter for three centuries there poured from Europe a continuous stream of friars and priests, who marched beside the explorers, erected monasteries in the regions brought under Spanish control, and established missions on the frontiers. For the mission was a frontier institution destined to do pioneer work in Christianizing and civilizing, according to the standards of Europe, the natives of the territory Spain was adding to her domains.

Music was soon found to be an important means in achieving this purpose. The early missionaries reported that the Indians in practically every region responded quickly to music. In order to avail themselves of this means of peaceful approach, they asked the king to furnish singers and instrument players who should accompany expeditions into hostile territory. In reply, the emperor Charles V, who was also the king of Spain, commanded the church authorities, for the Church controlled all education in those days, to furnish musicians wherever needed, in order to further the purposes of the Spanish crown. To supply musicians, it was necessary to teach the natives. The first teacher of European music in North America was Fray Pedro de Gante, who established a school in Mexico City in 1527, and at once made music one of the most important subjects of the curriculum, for musicians were needed in the services of the Church as well as in missionary projects.* Soon monasteries dotted the Valley of Mexico and then the regions

---

*L. Spell, "The First Teacher of European Music in America," in *Catholic Historical Quarterly*, New Series, II (1923), 372-378.

westward to the Pacific; in all these there were teachers of music who taught the young Indians not only to sing and play but also how to construct all the instruments then known in Europe. Rapidly the line of missions was moved northward; by 1600 the Spanish frontier line had reached the Rio Grande. From the adjacent regions the missionaries drew the Indians with whom they labored in their efforts at civilization; some of these were from the wandering Texas tribes.

An entirely different purpose had brought the Spaniards to that stream much earlier. The Spanish leaders, the famed *conquistadores*, dreamed of finding gold and other treasures, of becoming fabulously wealthy over night. Hardly had they made themselves masters of the Aztec territory when strange tales came to their ears of gold in the "great unknown North"; always lured by hopes of riches without labor, a band of intrepid explorers crossed the Rio Grande and pushed on into what is today New Mexico. The point at which they crossed they called by the Spanish word for ford, "El Paso." But the expected treasure was not found; only the homes of the cliff-dwellers met their disappointed gaze. That group returned to the fertile valleys of the Aztecs, but New Mexico was not forgotten. Before the end of the century other expeditions had gone north with colonists, cattle, and supplies to establish permanent settlements in the territory Coronado and his band had explored.

It was as an approach to those settlements in New Mexico that the first mision was established near the present city of El Paso in 1659. There the first European music known in Texas was taught to the Indian boys who were gathered within the sheltering walls by a kindly missionary fired with the hope of civilizing them. Friar García de San Francisco, who established this mission of Our Lady of Guadalupe, had previously worked in the missions in New Mexico and had built an organ for the chapel of each one he served. While we have no definite statement that he did the same for the Texas mission in which he worked until 1671, it is probable that he built the first organ used on Texas soil; we know that while training his boys to live like civilized people he taught them to sing the songs and prayers of the church and to play on various other instruments.* That the mission did not grow

---

*L. Spell, "Music Teaching in New Mexico in the Seventeenth Century," in *New Mexico Historical Review*, II (1927).

into a famous one is possibly due to the troubles that followed in New Mexico; in 1680 the Indians by a prearranged plan all rose in rebellion, and killed or drove back across the Rio Grande every Spaniard in the territory. Then, for a time, they were free once more.

The Spaniards proved themselves earnest and determined people, especially in trying to Christianize the natives of the New World. With the Mendoza expedition, which penetrated as far as San Angelo, came Father López, bringing with him a portable organ. On this he produced music which amazed the Indians. This instrument is the first of the organ family specifically named in the records of Texas. Other expeditions crossed the Rio Grande further south, and some made settlements. Over along the Trinity River was a tribe of Indians called the Tejas; they were said to be docile. Before the end of the seventeenth century the missionaries were at work among these natives, from whom it is said comes the name of the state. But before much progress in civilizing them could be made, the imminence of the French caused the Spanish authorities to abandon these missions and establish others further west. The sites chosen for the most famous of the Texas missions, five of which still stand, were along the San Antonio River. This was far enough west to bring the missionaries in touch with the nomadic plains tribes which crossed Texas according to the seasons—in the fall they went south to Mexico; in the spring they turned north. The missionaries tried to persuade them to live in one place, to learn the principles of the Christian religion, and to work. They tried to induce them to want better homes, food and clothes, and to teach them other ways of amusing themselves than fighting, getting drunk, and eating other human beings. Father Solís reported on the work of the father in charge at the Mission Rosario:

Each Saturday he calls them together and has them recite the Rosary, with the various mysteries, and has them sing the *Alabado.* Before Mass on Sunday and feast days he makes them recite their prayers and the lessons of the catechism, and afterward he preaches and explains to them the Christian doctrine. . . .*

But most of the Texas Indians loved freedom more than civiliza-

---

*"The Solís Diary of 1767," in *Preliminary Studies of the Texas Catholic Historical Society*, I (March, 1931), No. 6, 20-21

tion, which implies both routine and labor; lured by beads, trinkets, food, and music, they would come into the mission and stay awhile; then they would run away and strike the trail again. Those who stayed learned many of the manual arts; through their labor the missions near San Antonio were built of stone, enlarged, and beautified; as they learned methods of irrigation, garden spots extended along the river; and under their care the herds of cattle grew large and prosperous. In the mission the Indian women did the cooking, spinning, and weaving. Each mission was soon an institution in which the necessities of life were produced.

In the daily life of the mission, music played an important part. At dawn there were matins; before the day's work was begun and at meal time there were prayers; at evening there were vespers. On Sunday and feast days there were the other regular services of the church. At all of these, there was music, the prayers being taught to the Indians set to very simple tunes, sometimes a native chant. Usually both prayers and hymns were taught responsively; the men and women assembled in the courtyard were divided into groups, one of which sang a line of a prayer or hymn, then the other followed with the same. All learned to sing the *Pater Noster*, the *Salve*, and the *Ave*; some of the more gifted were taught to sing more elaborate chants and hymns and to play on such instruments as the guitar, flute, and violin. There are no organs mentioned in the existing reports of the activities in the missions along the San Antonio River, but the music at San Juan, which was founded in 1718, was unusually good, for Father Solís reported in 1767:

All of these Indians speak Spanish. . . . .Most of them play some musical instrument, the guitar, the violin or the harp. All have good voices, and on Saturdays, the 19th of each month and on the feasts of Our Lord and of the Blessed Virgin they take out their rosaries, while a choir of four voices, soprano, alto, tenor and bass, with musical accompaniment, sings so beautifully that it is a delight to hear it. . . . . Both men and women can sing and dance just as the Spaniards, and they do so, perhaps, even more beautifully and more gracefully.*

One of the first hymns sung in Texas, according to tradition, was the *Alabado*, introduced by Fray Margil de Jesús,

*Ibid, 21.

(9)

PATER NOSTER

GREGORIAN CHANT

FIG. 1

one of the earliest of the missionaries to Texas. When his group reached a point a few miles north of the center of the present city of San Antonio, they were exhausted, hungry and thirsty. They had travelled over a long stretch of territory without finding any prospect of water. In the heat of a Texas sun, it was a simple matter to become parched, and their water supply was exhausted. But the courage of the leader never flagged, although his companions had lost heart completely. Resting under a large tree, Fray Margil happened to look up and spied a vine from whose branches hung luscious grapes. In trying to reach some of these he gave the vines a tug that

AN OLD *ALABADO*

A-la-ba-do y en-sal-za--do   Se a el di-vi--no Sa---cra-men-to;

En quien Dios o-cul-to a-sis-te   De las al-mas el   sus-ten-to.

Let us sing the praises and glories
Of what the Sacrament can avail us,
Let us sing that God in person comes
To stay the spirits that fail us.

FIG. 2

uprooted them; at once a great jet of water spurted forth. As the amazed men quickly gathered about the spring, they found other smaller springs had also broken through; and soon the water was trickling off into a beautiful little winding stream. This the group dedicated to St. Anthony; and on the banks of that stream the city of San Antonio was later founded. In praise of God, who had cared for them in such bountiful fashion, all fell on their knees and sang the *Alabado,* which was later learned by all the neophytes in the mission. Various texts are known; the last stanza attributed to Margil is the following:

He who wishes to follow God
And enter into his kingdom,
One thing must declare
And say with all his heart:
"To die rather than to sin,
Rather than to sin, to die."

Some glimpses of the life and customs of the Indians in the missions are given by a volume written by Bartolomé García, a missionary at San Francisco de la Espada from 1750 to 1760.* The numerous shortcomings of the natives were usually attri-

*For further details see the writer's "The First Textbook Used in Texas," in *The Southwestern Historical Quarterly,* XXIX (1926) 289-295.

ALABADO AS SUNG IN TEXAS TODAY

A-la-ba-do sea el San-ti --si-mo Sacra-mento del al-tar Y la

Virgen con-ce - - bida Sin pe - - ca-do o - - - ri - gi - - nal.

Sea en cielo y en la tierra
Alabado sin cesar

El corazón amoroso
Que hasta mí quiere llegar.

Sing praises, sing of the
Sacrament,
Its solemn consecration,
Sing praises, sing Mary the
Virgin
Of sinless generation.

Now both in Heav'n and upon the
earth
May praises ring unending
Of that compassionate Master
That over us is bending.

Fig. 3

buted by them either to laziness or forgetfulness. Their insistent belief in the meaning of the hoot of an owl, the song of a bird, the cry of an animal, or dreams and evil spirits gave the missionaries much concern. Then the Indian persisted in cursing; especially when lying, angry, or doing wrong, he invoked the name of God, the cross, the Virgin Mary, and all the saints of his acquaintance. He was not always an enthusiastic church-goer; sometimes when he attended mass he fell into a blissfully somnolent attitude. Fasting had small appeal for him; instead he reveled in human flesh, and in drinking a concoction made from *peyote* or the laurel beans, both of which served as narcotics. Furthermore the Indian danced and sang his own songs, many of which did not find favor with the church fathers. The *mitote* especially appealed to the natives, who contended it was an innocent diversion; while the missionaries said it was heathen, superstitious, and dangerous, for it was always danced at drunken revels. Clearly the native dances and songs were too closely associated with the Indian's own forms of religion for them to be generally acceptable in the Christian chapel. The fact that the Indians persisted in using their own songs and dances reveals how deep-rooted some of their traditions and practices were.

The missions were supported as homes for the Indians until 1794; by that time it seemed to the Spanish government that the natives should be sufficiently civilized to be given lands and permitted to live in homes of their own. Religious services were continued in the chapels; but priests served instead of the friars. In the century the Texas missions functioned, many devoted churchmen dedicated their lives to the Indians; of the various subjects taught them, music was, throughout the period, one which received most attention. In the records of these institutions we find references to Indians who became especially proficient in some branch of music; these were frequently sent to other missions to serve as instructors of their red brethern. Some few Gregorian tunes used in those days are still known to descendants of those Indians. But long before the missions were secularized, other people had come to carry forward the use and perpetuation of Spanish music of another type.

CHAPTER III

Spanish-Mexican Folk Music

AT the time the missions were founded, the Spanish government sent small detachments of troops to establish garrisons or forts nearby as a protection against encroaching foreigners and hostile Indians. It was not long before some of these men brought their families and perhaps friends to live near them; in that way settlements were made in Texas near the missions long before such were officially recognized. Not until the Spaniards were alarmed over reports that the French were about to occupy Texas did the government send colonists to make permanent homes in the province. A few miles from the head of the river to which Fray Margil had given the name of San Antonio, settlers from the Canary Islands laid out in 1731 a town which they called San Antonio de Béxar. As soon as houses were built, these people, who were all Catholics, set about the construction of a church. This became the cathedral of San Fernando, which still faces Main Plaza. During the rule of Texas by Spain and Mexico, this church boasted neither an organ nor a large choir. San Antonio was a poor, struggling settlement. The only music heard in the church was that furnished by a small group of boys, who were trained by the parish priest. The services in the church of San Fernando were as simple as in the mission chapels, which the citizens often attended.

As a distraction from the toil and hardships of pioneer life in this Spanish city in Texas, music was the one art which could serve, for books and pictures were scarce. The Spanish people had been for centuries music-loving; they sang at their work, and sang and danced as recreation in their leisure hours. The Isleños, as the Canary Island settlers were called, brought with them the songs and dances they had learned in their former homes. Many of the songs of old Spain, some peculiar to the Canary Islands, and others of distinctly Indian origin from Mexico were thus introduced during the eighteenth century by new settlers who from time to time joined the struggling little colony at San Antonio. Among these were the songs of the chariot-eer, for all supplies had to be brought overland from Mexico either mule-back or by the painfully slow ox-cart; the songs of the plowman, as his ox-drawn plow leisurely broke the virgin soil; the songs of the wine-maker, whose vineyards stretched from the San Antonio to the San Pedro or from one bend of the river to another, watered by the winding *acequias;* and the songs of the women as they ground their corn, Indian-style, on the *metate,* or rocked their babies to sleep. From

LULLABY OF A SPANISH MOTHER

Se-ño-ra Sant' An - - na   Why's the ba - by   cry - ing?

Is it for an   ap - ple   That you've been de - - - ny - - ing?

We'll go to the garden,   One for the Christ Child
There we will pull two   And one for you.

Señora Sant' Ana,   Vamos a la huerta,
¿ Por qué llora el niño?   Cortaremos dos,
Por una manzana   Una para el Niño,
Que se le ha perdido?   Otra para vos.

FIG. 4

one or more of these same sources came the tunes of the street venders—those picturesque figures which early made their appearance in Texas and soon became very numerous, for everything salable was peddled from house to house; merchandizing on an infinitely small scale was a favorite occupation of both men and women, and has continued so until the 20th century. There were the venders of wood and water; these bore their goods at first on their backs, later in two-wheeled carts or on donkey-back. Water for household consumption was sold to those who did not live directly along the stream; and wood and charcoal packed on the patient burro are still familiar wares in the Mexican section of San Antonio. Later came the venders of *tamales* and *masa;* still later those of pastries and

CALL OF THE *TAMALE* VENDER

¿No to-ma-rán ta-ma-les ca- · · -lien-tes tor-ti-llas con chi-le?
Don't you want ta-ma-les, hot, hot, hot ones? Tor-ti-llas with chi-le?

FIG. 5

sweets. From time to time all the knicknacks so dear to the heart of women were harked from door to door or rather from window to window, for much of the bargaining went on through the grated windows, and only on rare occasions were the venders invited to enter the patio of the house. Some of the Indian foods early known in the Spanish settlements in Texas were the *tortillas,* the *tamale, chile con carne,* and *frijoles.* This can readily be understood as both corn and beans could generally be depended upon for a crop. The *tamale* vender with his *tortillas* kept warm in the upper compartment of his charcoal-heated *tamale* container was a familiar figure. Sometimes he carried two containers; in this case he had *chile* also for sale. Each day about sunset his familiar call might be heard as he passed leisurely through the narrow streets.

Every evening that the weather was at all propitious one could depend upon hearing a steady stream of music on the plaza.* On one side of the square were the stands at which cooked food was dispensed; under the light of old Spanish lanterns, on tables erected each evening of long boards placed on saw-horses, suppers of *tamales, tortillas* and *chile* were served to eager patrons. Nearby lolled a singer who strummed his guitar as an accompaniment, sometimes there was a small group of singers, each playing some instrument. Here one heard not the brief call of the vender, but the interminable *romance,* some old ballad strung out to unbelievable length,

---

*Military Plaza first served; much later Alamo Plaza for a while; now the stands are on the Market Square, near the grave of Ben Milam.

frequently extended or colored by the imagination of the singer. To the same tune many verses were monotonously chant-
ed. Around these tables gathered all social classes; all were
familiar with the tales of sixteenth-century Spain. Here
one heard of the strange happenings on St. John's Day so long
ago; of the soldier who returned from the war only to discover the inconstancy of his lady; the story of Preste Juan of
the Indies; and many others. No doubt the prisoners in the
old *calabozo* which was located across the corner from the old
governor's palace, enjoyed the bits of song wafted to their ears
as much as those lodged in more spacious quarters. On the
other plaza, now known as Main, another practice kept music
alive in the midst of these settlers. As soon as the community
boasted a number of string players, a small orchestra was
formed. In pleasant weather these players dispensed music
on the plaza. Around the walk on the outside of the square
the elder people sat and chatted, while the younger promenaded, the girls in one direction, the youths in the opposite,
thus making possible frequent meetings and side glances, if
not a few words. For the Spanish or Mexican girl was guard-
ed quite as carefully in Texas as in medieval Spain. After
the settlement boasted players of brass instruments, a band
played on the plaza and, later, on the Alameda—a park extending back from the river about where East Commerce Street is
now. On Sunday in the summer, the leading families assembled
there in the late afternoons. Dancing was a common diversion in the homes; at first the music was sung to a guitar accompaniment; later the violin, harp, and flute lent their aid.
Until the twentieth century these Mexican orchestras continued in demand for dances among the whole population; they
still exist in the Mexican group.

Some of the customs in connection with the celebration of
Christmas kept Spanish tunes alive in Texas. One of these
was the *posadas,* given usually on any of the nine nights preceding Christmas and culminating in the *Nacimiento* on Christmas Eve; another was the *pastores,* a slight dramatic performance given on various evenings before Christmas and often
as late as Epiphany or Twelfth Night. For the *posadas,* a
form of entertaining a small group of friends by commemorat-
ing the struggle of Mary to find lodgings as the time approached

(17)

for the birth of her baby, the inside of a room or a patio was converted into the semblance of a wood by the use of boughs of cedar or other foliage. Candles or crude paper lanterns were suspended in various places. First, everyone present knelt and sang a hymn, usually the Litany of the Virgin; then all formed a procession at the head of which marched the tiny children with their little candles; then came the young people, also with candles; then the elders who were followed by a group of children carrying on their shoulders the figures of the Blessed Pilgrims, with the angels and the indispensable little mule, arranged on some kind of a background which suggested the cold of a winter's night. After these came such players of guitars and flutes as were available, while the family servants brought up the rear. Sometimes the children bearing the figures led. After proceeding through the patio or several rooms, the singers separated into groups, one of which returned with the rest of the company to the inside of the decorated room; the other remained with the children bearing the figures on the outside. Then began the appeal for shelter:

De lar-ga jor-na- -da Ren-di- -dos lle-ga- -mos

Y casi lo implo-ra- - -mos Pa- -ra des-can-sar.

From long and weary journey,
Forspent, alone and harried,
Here by your door we tarried,
But to beg that we may rest us here.

(18)

To which those inside answered:

Quién a nuestras puertas	Who is it braves the darkness,
En noche inclemente	The storm that rages coldly,
Se acerca imprudente	Who comes and calls so boldly,
Para molestar?	And disturbs the hour of homely cheer?

After repeated appeals from outside, those inside made known their intentions to admit the suppliants:

Entrad, pues !oh esposos!	Then enter, worthy Joseph
Castos e inocentes,	And Mary, pure and holy,
Cultos y reverentes	Our household which though lowly
Venid a aceptar.	Will receive and shelter and revere.

Then rejoicing from the outside rose to its height:

Abranse las puertas,	Now rend the veils that hide him,
Rómpanse los velos,	Throw open all the portals
Que viene a posar	ᵀor he is coming, mortals,
El Rey de los cielos.	Lo, the King of Heav'n is drawing near.

With much commotion, they burst in and placed the figures on a table. Then all knelt and said the prayer for the day, ending with seven Ave Marias, each of which was concluded by:

FIG. 6

Lovely pilgrim coming from above
O Mary, bearing grace,
In my heart are walls and a roof of love
For your earthly dwelling-place.

(19)

After the song was finished, general merriment reigned and refreshments of some kind were served.

On Christmas Eve the *Nacimiento* was given. This portrayed dramatically the happenings near Bethlehem. On an improvised stage were Joseph and Mary kneeling on each side of the cradle; at the front or on each side were the ass and the mule; and always present were the three Wise Men, the first represented as a Spaniard, the second as an Indian, and the third as a negro. Over the door hung an angel supporting with her hands the emblem *Gloria in excelsis deo;* above shone the sky, depicting a long comet, representing that which guided the steps of the three Wise Men to the birth place. Shepherds and shepherdesses entered and told their story of watching the stars and following to find at last the manger and the Child. At the end, all joined in singing cradle songs and Christmas carols.*

Closely connected with the Manger Scene of Christmas Eve were the *pastores*—slight dramatic productions of the same events but emphasizing also the eternal struggle between good and evil. In these little plays there was always a devil of some description which delayed the journey, caused minor disasters along the way, or prevented the couple from finding lodgings. To those who did not sense beneath the surface of the plot, this character represented only the comic element; it also gave opportunity for amusing songs, often at most incongruous moments. In the *pastorelas* there were always many inconsistencies either in the background, the garb of the characters, or in minor details. A distinguishing feature, however, were the songs, largely old Spanish words and melodies, kept alive through repeated use with the children each year. These performances, which were crude indeed in the early days of the settlements in Texas, still continue in the Mexican sections of the larger cities and in the border towns, the number of performances often being determined by the need for the proceeds derived therefrom.

Other tunes were kept alive through children's games. One of these is *La Viudita,* sung as a circle game. In the center

---

*One of the most beautiful is to be found in the Texas Centennial Edition of the *Music Hour* (p. xiv), published by Silver, Burdett & Co.

Yo soy la viu di ta del con de Lau rel y quie .-ro c a
Young countess and widow Am I of Laurel, And I would re

sarme, y no sé con quien y no se con quién
marry— But whom I can't tell. But whom I can't tell.

FIG. 7

.Pues siendo tan bella   Since, lady so charming,
no tienes con quien,   No husband you find,
escoge a tu gusto,   Come choose from our hundreds
aquí tienes cien.   The one to your mind.

Escojo a Carmelo,   I choose, then, Carmelo,
por ser la más gentil   As handsome and gay,
y pura azucena   The fairest of flowers
de Mayo a Abril.   From June until May.

of the ring is the *viudita,* who selects in turn her successor. In one form or another, and set to various tunes, this game is known throughout the Spanish world.

It is to be regretted that more of the secular music of the Spanish and Mexican settlers of Texas has not been recorded. The love of music and dancing was a part of their heritage throughout the Southwest; in these regions the folk songs of sixteenth and seventeenth-century Spain were long kept alive. Descendants of both Spaniards and Indians were skilled both in playing and in making guitars and flutes; particularly did they excel in group playing of stringed instruments.

Interest in the music bequeathed to Texas by the Spaniards is just beginning to awaken. The Spanish folk tales and folk songs are now the subject of extensive research; the *romances* or ballads are being collected and eagerly studied by specialists. With this newly aroused enthusiasm will come a more general realization that the Spaniards were the pioneers of music in Texas. They introduced European music through the missions; they furnished the first music teacher, out in the west where the Rio Grande was first forded by Europeans; and long before music was brought westward from the Atlantic coast, Texas knew the solemn chants and hymns of the Catholic church as well as the folk music of Spain. While New England was singing psalm tunes, rhythms reminiscent of the Moors and melodies tinged with Mexican melancholy were a part of the cultural heritage of the descendants of the Spanish and Mexican settlers in Texas.

CHRISTMAS CAROL

Jubilosamente	Joyous, O most joyous
Vén y adora amante	Come and bow before Him,
El divino infante	Love Him and adore Him,
Pequeñito Dios.	Him the infant God,
Por él está el cielo	Him for whom the heavens,
Sembrado de estrellas,	Starry-bright with wonder,
Por él son tan bellas	Shine above and under
Las obras de Dios.	Goodly works of God.

CHAPTER IV

Anglo-American Music

WHILE life moved on uneventfully in the few Spanish settlements in Texas—San Antonio, Goliad, Nacogdoches and Salcedo on the Trinity were the only ones sufficiently important in 1805 to be put on the map—strange things were happening in Europe. Many of the changes were due to Napoleon, who after arousing the admiration of all those who dreamed of a republic and democracy, made himself the emperor of France. When most of western Europe had been conquered, he decided to add Spain to his realm, and very soon his troops were invading that peninsula. While the people there were busy fighting the French soldiers, the Spanish colonists in the New World found it a propitious moment to follow the example of the United States and become independent. As a result, when Mexico accomplished this, Texas found herself no longer a Spanish province, but a part of a Mexican state. Those in charge of the government in Mexico City, the capital, found that is was not so easy to govern a people who had never before known much freedom. Among the acts of the new government that Mexico bitterly regretted later was the privilege granted to a few people from the United States to make settlements of Anglo-Americans in Texas. For, as soon as this permission was granted, English-speaking people from the United States began to pour over the border. Between 1822 and 1836 they opened roads, built towns, and slowly drove the Indians back. Although they promised when they came to use the Spanish language and to be good Catholics, they did neither very long. They were not accustomed to the slow, tedious way of doing business that the Spaniards had taught the Mexicans; and they were soon determined to manage their affairs more quickly and in their own way.

The Anglo-Americans who settled in Texas held conflicting views in regard to music; these varied somewhat according to the social class. Some of the colonists were people of wealth, for whom playing and singing were common forms of diversion. Such a man was Colonel Jared Groce, who arrived with fifty or more wagons; in some of these the women and children travelled; in others came the furniture, spinning wheels and looms, and provisions for many months. On horseback were the men driving other horses, mules, cows, sheep, and hogs. Such people built large, comfortable homes and cleared extensive tracts of land; they became the leaders in industry and government. Among the other things they brought into Texas were musical instruments; and usually among their slaves were some accustomed to furnish music for dancing and other forms of entertainment.

It was as a rule the poor settler that regarded music as the work of the devil. Men of this class had little equipment, little education, and few home diversions. Their only contact with music had been through the church; and even there it was not regarded very favorably. Dancing was an unforgivable sin. While some of the more prosperous class shared these views, it was almost uniformly true that the "poor white" was antagonistic to music except that suggestive of psalm tunes. But however the two social classes differed in their views regarding music and dancing, they were as one in their attitude toward the Mexican government; they were ambitious, energetic, active and determined in their opposition to the whole Spanish system.

In the clash of the Anglo-Americans and the Mexicans— groups differing in language, laws and customs, and religion— the natural result was that as the Anglo-Americans became more numerous than the Spanish-speaking settlers, the newcomers became the rulers. The Mexican government sent an army into Texas to enforce the laws; but it was useless. On March 2, 1836, the Texans declared their independence from Mexico. After the battle of the Alamo—one of the old missions, San Antonio de Valero, converted into a fortress—at which nearly every American was killed on March 6, 1836, and the massacre at Goliad,—the Texans were thoroughly aroused. Sam Houston hastily raised an army on the Brazos, met the Mexicans on April 21 at San Jacinto and defeated them completely, taking the Mexican president, Santa Anna, prisoner. At that battle the musicians played "Yankee Doodle" and "Will you come to the Bower," a song written

WILL YOU COME TO THE BOWER?

Will you come to the bower I have shad — ed for you? I've decked it with ros - - - es all spangled with dew.

Will you, will you will you, will you Come to my bower? Will you will you, will you.. will you, Come to my bower?

> There, under the bower, on roses you'll rest,
> While a smile lights the eyes of the girl I love best.
>> Will you, will you, will you, will you,
>> Smile, my beloved?
>
> But the roses so fair will not rival your cheek
> Nor the dew be so sweet as the vows we shall speak.
>> Will you, will you, will you, will you,
>> Speak, my beloved?
>
> We'll swear mid the roses we never shall part
> Thou fairest of roses, thou queen of my heart.
>> Will you, will you, will you, will you,
>> Won't you, my love?

FIG. 8

by Thomas Moore, but which soon became known in Texas both as "The Invitation" and "The San Jacinto Quickstep,"

THE INVITATION*

Will you come to the battlefield we've chosen for you?
Your reception shall be bloody—your runaways but few.
Come, come, oh come, we dare you to the battle.
Ye Mexicans so brave—Santa Anna at your head,
Jacinto's fields, perchance, again shall fatten with your dead.
Then come with all your prison hoard of wretches on our borders,
We'll teach them how to march, in quick time, without orders.
When next your President we catch, a-hiding in our bushes,
We'll give him, what he should have had, sans pity, sans excuses.
You have blustered long enough with your talk about invasion,
You had better come in earnest now upon the first occasion.
We'll meet you, and we'll greet you, with sound of pipe and drum
Will you come to the battle—will you come—will you come?

Sung to the tune of *Will You Come to the Bower*, the charge at San Jacinto.

and was shortly proclaimed the "national song of the Republic of Texas." The only instruments they had were drums, fifes,

*From the *San Luis Advocate* Jan 29, 1841. Printed on Galveston Island by the first printer in Texas, Samuel Bangs.

clarions or bugles, and cymbals, but they played right lustily as the troops went into action. Among these musicians were Thomas Wesson, John N. Beebe and Peter Allen; one of the fifers is said to have been Frederick Limsky, a Czech; and George Broom was a drummer. Some of these musicians were later rewarded by the republic of Texas with lands and a pension for their good work on that spring morning. The success of the battle gave rise to quite a flood of patriotic music; seven more or less original poems appeared in the lone newspaper of the period, *The Texas Telegraph*. Two of these "Texians to your Banner Fly" and "Texians Brave" were set to the tune of "Scots what hae with Wallace Bled;" two others, "The Texian War Cry" and "Hymn of the Alamo" were sung to the melody of the *Marseillaise;* "The Battle of San Jacinto" employed the tune of *Yankee Doodle* for the main stanzas and "The Hunters of Kentucky" for the chorus; while the "Song of the Texian Prisoner in Mexico" utilized the melody of "Days of Absence." Another song popular at that era, the words of which appeared in the press, was "The Banks of the Blue Moselle" (Fig. 10).

By the time Texas became an independent nation, many musical instruments and music books had been brought into Texas by Anglo-American settlers, some few of whom were musicians. Among the pioneer music teachers of the period were two young women, Mrs. Wightman, the wife of a surveyor at Matagorda, and Miss Frances Trask, a member of a prominent Boston family. The honor of being the first woman composer among the Anglo-Americans in Texas probably falls to Mary Holley, a cousin of Stephen F. Austin; she wrote,

NEW GOODS.— The subscriber has just landed from New-Orleans, with an assortment of Goods for this market, of which the following is a part:
HARDWARE AND CUTLERY.—Corn Mills; coffee do.; cross-cut, pit and hand-saws; hoes; trace and ox chains; cast steel axes; froes; foot adzes; hatchets; chisels; augurs; gimblets; drawing knives;bolts;hinges; screws; butcher, dirk, pocket and pen knives; knives and forks; razors and strops; German Harps; spurs; brass candlesticks; snuffers; brass stirrups; plated do.;violin strings; rifle flints, etc.
R. J. MOSELEY.
March 12.—4tf.

German harps for sale by R. J. Moseley at San Felipe de Austin. This is the first mention of a musical instrument in the Texas press. It appears in *The Mexican Citizen,* one of the earliest newspapers printed in Texas (1831).

FIG. 9

(26)

THE BANKS OF THE BLUE MOSELLE

G. H. B. Rodwell

FIG. 10

while visiting in the province, that she had composed a boat-
song on the Brazos in 1831, and tells entertainingly in her let-
ters of young Zavala, who sang and played the piano and the guitar, while other Mexicans and Americans sang and played the flute, guitar, violin, and accordion. As with the Spanish settlers, among the Anglo-Americans dancing was a favorite form of recreation. Often negroes were the fiddlers; but a Mr. Choate is remembered as one of the early settlers who fiddled for dances. When Sam Houston became president, a grand ball was held in Houston, at which all the best fiddlers avail-

---

MUSIC.

The subscriber takes leave to inform the public generally, that from the first of February next he will teach Music in its various branches. Also the German and French languages, at his house, opposite to Mr. Cooke's store.   F. LEMKY.

Houston, Jan. 24, 1838.

INSTRUCTION ON THE FLUTE.—
Mr. Sames, (late of the principal northern theatres,)now member of the Houston theatre, begs respectfully to acquaint the citizens, that he proposes devoting a few hours in the day to giving instruction in the above delightful accompaniment, on the most approved principles and on the most liberal terms. Any commands left at Mr. King's, Star Coffee House, will be attended to. [Jan. 30, 1839]

Two notices of music teachers from the *Texas Telegraph*, published in Houston.

FIG. 11

---

able were assembled to furnish the music. Soon, according to the newspapers, there was a piano and flute teacher in Houston; music stools and a Spanish guitar were for sale; and a piano was auctioned off.

With the establishment of the capital of the new republic at Houston, that city became at once a center of social life. By 1838 a theater was opened there, for which a company of no mean ability was brought from the United States. The leader of the "full and efficient" orchestra, as well as its members, gave music lessons during the day, and, when not busy at the theater, played for dances at the hotels and in private homes. One of the favorite actresses, Madame Thielemann (Louise Ehlers, who prior to her marriage had been engaged at the royal theater in Cassel, Germany, and had played in New York, St. Louis, and New Orleans) was a popular singer, who delighted her audiences with such songs as "Does your Mother Know you're Out," "Come Dwell with Me,"

(27)

"Love was once a Little Boy," and the popular romance from *Fra Diavolo* "On Yonder Rock Reclining" (see page 102). On January 9, 1839, there was presented a "new national Texas hymn called the Texas Star" written by Mr. Corri, the manager of the theater.

THE FIRST CONCERT HALL IN TEXAS—THE CAPITOL OF THE REPUBLIC OF TEXAS, HOUSTON 1837.

FIG. 12

Concerts early became popular among the Anglo-Americans in Texas. The first capitol in Houston was used as a concert hall before it served its original purpose, and was used for concerts during many years. One of the pioneers in the long list of singers, varying in type from negro minstrels to European exiles, who introduced the best of foreign music was Mrs. De Bar, some of whose programs are published in the local press of the day. Local singing organizations also gave concerts.

> Mrs. Debar commences her concerts at the Capitol on Wednesday Evening next, assisted by Mr. Debar, Archer and an Amateur. From the bills we have no doubt that the public will be delightfully entertained.
>
> Announcement of first public concerts in Houston. From the *Morning Star* May 28, 1839.
>
> FIG. 13

The attitude toward and the contribution to music of the

(28)

Anglo-American church in Texas was both positive and negative. In 1838 a "monthly concert prayer meeting" was held in the capitol in Houston. There was also a sacred music society which rehearsed in the capitol; later, after the seat of government had

There will be preaching in the Senate Chamber next Sabbath, at the usual hours. Sunday School at nine o'clock.

The Monthly Concert Missionary Prayer Meeting, will be held at the same place next Monday evening. Service to commence at seven o'clock.

FIG. 14

been transferred, a similar organization was formed in Austin. Not until 1848 was a good church organ brought to Texas; that was shipped from New Orleans by order of Bishop Odin and installed in the Catholic church in Galveston, at the cost of $2,000. But there were many ministers and church members who bitterly opposed any form of music, and their influence prevented the encouragement of the art in various communities. The conference which selected the Methodist missionaries for Texas passed a resolution in 1838 that "The introduction of instrumental music and the conducting of music in our churches by choirs is injurious to the spirituality of singing and is inconsistent with the directions of our Disciples." And in 1840 a Methodist preacher was complaining that the prospects for a good revival in Austin had been destroyed by a dancing school. Such an attitude did not favor the promotion of music in either religious or secular life. As a result we find such doggerel hymns as that sung by a pious old lady down on Caney Creek:

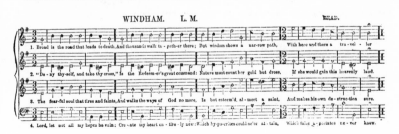

WINDHAM. L. M.

1. Broad is the road that leads to death, And thousands walk together there; But wisdom shows a narrow path, With here and there a traveler

2. "Deny thyself, and take thy cross," Is the Redeemer's great command: Nature must count her gold but dross, If she would gain this heavenly land.

3. The fearful soul that tires and faints, And walks the ways of God no more, Is but esteem'd, al-most a saint, And makes his own destruction sure.

4. Lord, let not all my hopes be vain; Cre-ate my heart en-tire-ly new: Which hypocrites could ne'er at-tain, Which false a-postates re-ver knew.

FIG. 15

The original form in which this tune appeared in singing school texts.

(29)

WINDHAM
As sung on Caney Creek

A Method ist it is my name;I hope to live and die the same;And

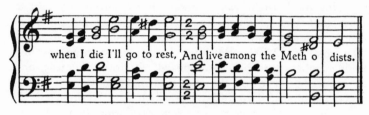

when I die I'll go to rest, And live among the Meth o dists.

The devil hates the Methodists
Because they sing and shout the best,
And when I die I'll go to rest,
And live among the Methodists.

FIG. 16

Out of the attitude that tolerated music only as an adjunct of the church grew two institutions which have survived in Texas life. The first of these was the singing school, that product of New England religious zeal. Instituted by religious leaders solely for the purpose of training adults to furnish music for the services of the church, the singing school by the beginning of the nineteenth century had so gained public favor that it was in some cases supported by local funds; its subject matter slowly and imperceptibly shifted from religious to secular music; its membership from the old to the young, both male and female; and the teachers were individuals who depended upon the fees for a livelihood. Its popularity spread westward with the moving frontier; it had reached the Mississippi early in the nineteenth century. Scarcely had the Anglo-Americans established themselves in the northeastern regions of Texas before the singing school had come, not in its most advanced stage, but in the primitive form that early New England had known it. It has survived almost a century.

As an outgrowth of the singing school in the various localities came the singing convention, a gathering of local singing societies in competitive meets at some convenient point. The Eastern Texas Vocal Musical Convention met in 1858 "on the Thursday before the third Sabbath in October. . . at the Christian Church on the Saline Road, six miles west of Camden in Rusk Co.," the *Galveston News* announced, copying from the *Henderson Beacon*. In these conventions, still common in many parts of the state, the religious element has always been predominant; in the early days it prevailed exclusively; and only with many misgivings are secular songs permitted to invade the sacred precincts of a singing convention still. The leader with a thunderous voice has been a typical factor; the singing-books still carry the shaped notes—a profitable commercial line, especially in East Texas; and the groups of eager if unlearned singers are at no pains to conceal the fact that the social aspect of the meeting is a strong drawing card. For the singing convention was no trifling affair; it lasted, in some cases, two or three days; and brought together members of widely scattered communities. There were always "good eats"—picnic fashion; sometimes a barbecue gave added zest to the appetite; usually each family brought food enough for three, and all was spread in community style. The books used might serve as an index to the westward advance of the publishing business; at first those used were printed in New England; then Philadelphia publications served; Cincinnati and New Orleans claimed the market after the middle of the century; now Arkansas and Texas promoters of musical progress turn the profits to their own pockets. On the shelves of many northeast Texas homes are to be found copies of the various volumes issued by Lowell Mason; while a late acquisition to the series is one *Roses of Spring,* issued as the mid-season offering of 1935, for new books each season contribute to the financial returns of the publishers.

The camp-meeting of the whites, first held in Texas in 1833, might in its later days be considered in some respects a projection of the singing convention. While the religious element was entirely predominant, so long as the institution survived music

(31)

played an important part.* Here the whole family came in a wagon; under the large tent, straw was spread thickly over the ground, and to its shelter slipped the babies, the children, and the adults when overcome by sleep. The camp-meeting songs were impregnated with the enthusiasm and religious zeal of the conductors; most of them sank deep in the hearts of those who heard and sang them. The railroad and the automobile have sounded the death-knell of the camp-meeting, except among the negroes; but some of the songs still live, as the collection made by Dean Meyer of Southwestern University attests.

Military music received some attention even in the early days. When the Santa Fé expedition was organized, John Doran went as sergeant major, and A. Pisarenski, Daniel B. Smith, and C. C. Willis were enlisted as musicians. It was the unhappy fate of the survivors of this expedition which gave rise to the song "The Santa Fé Prisoners," whose two stanzas were sung with zest to the tune of "Columbia, Land of Liberty."

> Americans, protect your blood,
>   From slavery's soul-galling chain,
> Shall brothers of fair freedom's sod,
>   Linger still in captive's pain?
> Shall foreign dungeons still confine,
>   The hearts that bled for freedom here?
> No, cross the mongrel Spaniard's line,
>   And by the blood of freedom swear
>   To rescue from captivity,
>   The prisoners of Santa Fe.
>
> Oh, shall it e'er be said that we,
>   Who hear their groans across the waves,
> Still suffered them to bow the knee,
>   To toil like brutes, and pine like slaves?
> Up, up, and strike the vengeful blow,
>   And for their liberation call,
> Or raze the lofty towers low,
>   And crush the tyrants in their fall,
>   And tear from vile captivity,
>   The prisoners of Santa Fe.

---

*Some typical songs of the Texas camp-meeting collected by Dean Henry E. Meyer are available in the *Publications of the Texas Folk Lore Society*, X (1932).

Meanwhile at Perote the Texans were solacing the slow hours by singing "A Soldier's Tear," "Will you come to the Bower," and "Long, long ago."

It was the treatment accorded these prisoners in Mexico as well as the boundary problem which arose with annexation that hastened the Mexican War. But before hostilities had begun, another factor in musical life had come upon the scene—the German settlers who were to play an important rôle in the cultivation of music in the next half century in Texas.

CHAPTER V

The Early German Contribution

IT would be hard to estimate the value of the German efforts to create and develop in Texas a love of good music. Musical people in their homeland and trained in the theory and practice of the art as were many of the leading emigrants, it was only natural that they should promote music in their new homes in the Southwest. Especially in Texas, where their largest settlements were rapidly made from 1845 on, was their influence strongly felt.

Of the Germans who entered the Republic before 1840, history records some evidences of a love of music. As early as 1834, when the Kleberg family arrived, they brought with them a good piano, which unfortunately perished in the burning of Harrisburg by Santa Anna. Mrs. Holley, a cousin of Stephen F. Austin, in writing from Galveston in 1837 of conditions in Texas commented on the Germans who "sang in concert."

After 1845 the number of Germans increased rapidly. Groups settled in Austin, La Grange, San Antonio, New Braunfels and Fredericksburg. Among those who came were trained musicians and instrument makers. In spite of the difficulties of pioneer life which beset them—Indians, lack of food, inadequate shelter, poor means of communication—these people bravely determined to wrest more than a mere existence from the wilds of Texas. In New Braunfels especially was the German spirit kept alive in song, and there in 1850 was formed the first German singing society in Texas. Soon other similar groups were organized in the neighboring German settlements. It was through the efforts of these groups, composed of men who met weekly for the practice of unaccompanied choral singing, that many of the works of the masters of music were first produced in Texas. From the individual groups, there was formed the Texas Saengerbund, or Singers' Union, which gave its first program at New Braunfels on October 15, 1853—the first saengerfest in the Southwest. Delegations from Sisterdale, Austin, and San Antonio attended. This saengerbund has continued to flourish until the present day with but two interruptions—the Civil War and the World War—and has done much to stimulate the efforts which resulted in the solid foundation of musical culture which is a characteristic of the German element in Texas today.

Of the many educated Germans who immigrated to Texas, Adolf Fuchs has a special interest for the history of music. A Lutheran pastor in Mecklenburg, he became interested in Texas through the account of travellers through the region, and decided to migrate there with a group organized for this purpose. At their departure for the New World, Hoffmann von Fallersleben, the famous poet, wrote a song honoring the occasion.

> On to Texas, on to Texas,
> Where the Lone Star in its glory,
> Prophecies a world of freedom,
> Beckons to each heart resounding
> To the call for truth and justice—
> There alone my heart would be.

This German poet who never saw Texas, wrote thirty other poems about life in Texas, copies of which Fuchs either brought with him or received later. Strange to say the title page gives the place of imprint as "San Felipe de Austin" and the publisher as "Adolf Fuchs and Company"—clearly a disguise for the benefit of the censor.

Texanische Lieder. Aus mundlicher und schriftlicher Mitteilung deutscher Texaner, mit sing weisen. San Felipe de Austin bei Adolf Fuchs & Co.

FIG. 17

Many of these poems Fuchs adapted to German folk-tunes; for others he composed the music. Fallersleben also wrote an opera, "In the Two Worlds," based on life in Texas.

After settling in the Brazos region, Adolf Fuchs taught for some years at the oldest girls' school now existing in Texas, Baylor College, established at that time at Independence. But he felt a longing for the hills, the broken country, and soon this master of five languages moved west to the Colorado River and settled in what is today Burnet County. Though he busied himself with farming and ranching problems, music never lost its interest. Until his death in 1885 he continued to compose; a manuscript volume preserved by the family is evidence of his creative bent. In this are songs of which he wrote both the words and the music and musical settings of poems by Fallersleben, Goethe, Uhland, and Wieland. While the volume

A GERMAN FOLKSONG

1. Kommt ein Vo-gel ge - flo-gen, setzt sich
2. Ach, so fern ist die Hei-mat, und so
3. Hab' mich all-weil ver - trö-stet auf die
4. Lie-ber Vo-gel, flieg' wei-ter, nimm ein'n

mf *Fine.*

nie - der auf mein'n Fuss, hat ein Brief-chen im Schna-bel, von der Mut-ter ein'n Gruss.
fremd bin ich hier, und es fragt hier kein Bru-der, kei-ne Schwester nach mir.
som-mer-li - che Zeit, und der Som-mer ist kom-men, und ich bin noch so weit.
Gruss mit und ein'n Kuss. Ach, ich kann dich nicht be - glei-ten, weil ich hier blei-ben muss.

D. C.

FIG. 18

To this melody (Figure 18) Fuchs adapted his translation of Fallersleben's poem "The German Backwoodsman."*

A rifle for hunting,
For defense or for fight,
A yoke of oxen for ploughing,
That is my delight.

My farm is enclosed,
My crop is laid by,
My log house is ready;
I laugh, I know why.

I sit on my pony,
Before me my gun,
Thus gaily through woods and
Through prairie I run.

A turkey I kill now,
A buck and a doe,
In lakes and in rivers
My line do I throw

I get bread from my cornfield
And meat from my sow,
From the spring I get water,
And milk from my cow.

I go hunting and chopping
Not fearing the dawn.
No keeper forbids me
The grape and pecan.

Nobody does trouble
My sheep and my geese,
They can feed about here
As much as they please.

Sometimes with the birds to
Sing songs I do chance,
Sometimes with the humbirds
The Fandango dance.

In the woods I feel happy
With my child and my wife,
But freedom is blessing
But freedom is life.

*Used by permission of the Adolf Fuchs Memorial Association.

possesses more historical than musical interest, it is ample evidence of the existence in Texas of a cultured man. He encouraged his children and his neighbors to sing; in his later years he held family reunions at which his own songs, in addition to those of the best German composers, were sung. Among his descendants are many who are musical; the best known is a grandson, Oscar Fox, who first achieved fame for his settings of Texas cowboy congs.

There were many German songs written in Texas before the Civil War; of these only the words have, in some cases, survived. The first was that composed by Count Solms-Braunfels on the occasion of the founding of New Braunfels (1845). It is said the verses were set to music by Alexis Bauer; others claim they were sung to a German folk-tune.* There is a *Festlied* written by Petmecky, the director of the Men's Singing Society "Liedertafel," organized in 1855, which begins "Texas hoch." Then we know of a Maennergesang by Adolf Douai, editor for a time of the *Frei Presse für Texas*, printed at San Antonio. There is an *Alamo Hymn* by C. Wilke, of which the words have been published; the music may still exist in the archives of the singing societies of New Braunfels.

Five years to a day after the opening of the first saengerfest in the Southwest (Oct. 15, 1858), there was born in Fredericksburg, then a frontier outpost, of a German mother and a Flemish father, a child who was destined to hold first rank among American musicians, Franz van der Stucken. His talent for music showed itself early and at the age of eight he was taken to Antwerp for a musical education, and enrolled as a pupil of Peter Benoit. While still a student there his compositions were played in the churches and a ballet by him was produced at the Royal Theater. In 1881 he became director of the Breslau City Theater, and, two years later, through the assistance of Liszt, he gave concerts of his own compositions at Weimar. In 1884 he was engaged to succeed Dr. Leopold Damrosch, who was director of the Arion Singing Society of NewYork. Very soon he became active as an orchestral director, conducting the Novelty Concerts of 1884 and 1885, the Symphony Concerts of 1886 and 1887, and the American Concerts of

*See Metzenthin-Raunick, S., *Deutsche Schriften in Texas* (1935)

the two following years. In 1895 he became director of the Cincinnati Conservatory and the Symphony Orchestra. He

FRANZ VAN DER STUCKEN

FIG. 19

conducted the May musical festivals there from 1906 to 1912 and again in 1923-25 and in 1927. In 1920 he directed the Wagner and Gluck revivals in Antwerp. His death occurred at Hamburg on August 16, 1929.

This Texas-born musician was among the first to recognize the genuine worth of American music. Not only did he try to foster it in the United States; he was the first conductor to tour Europe with an American group of singers presenting American songs. He encouraged young composers, and predicted the recognition which has since come, in some degree, to music created on this side of the Atlantic. Himself a prolific composer, he also devoted much time to orchestral and choral arrangements, one of the most extensive being his adaptation of the Bach Passion Music for presentation at one of the Cincinnati festivals. In this field his work is marked by the same depth and seriousness so evident in the other branches of creative art. In his later years he visited Texas and found both the state and Fredericksburg proud to claim him as a native son. During his seventy years of life he was showered with honors in recognition of the value of his contribution to the world of music. His name must, so far, head the list of the illustrious Germans born in the Southwest who have forged their way to the front rank in music.

In many lines of musical endeavor the Germans early became

(38)

At the Window

Maurice Thompson

Frank van der Stucken

I heard __ the wood - pec - ker tap - ping,

The blue - bird ten - der - ly sing; I

turned and look'd out of my win - dow, And lo! __

__ it was spring! __

FIG. 20

(40)

leaders. In Houston, Galveston, San Antonio and in the smaller places bands were formed of Germans and directed by Germans. Concerts by local and foreign talent were fostered; outstanding among the visiting groups were those of the German and Hungarian exiles driven from their homes by political conditions. Largely through German insistence, music was introduced into the first public schools established in the state—those in Galveston, in 1845; and early in the fifties a music teacher was employed by the public schools of San Antonio. Other communities in which the Germans were strong followed the example of these cities; even before the Civil War a good beginning had been made toward the musical education of the younger German generation. In the private schools in all parts of the state Germans quickly secured positions as music teachers and contributed largely to the musical education of the girls.

Among the early teachers was one who figured also as a composer—Gustave Fitze, whose compositions were published by Oliver Ditson & Co. Among these were "I Know Not Why I Love Thee" and the "Waverly" and "Starlight" schottisches. Mr. Fitze taught in Galveston, at Waverly, in Walker County, and at the Richmond Academy in Fort Bend County.

The commercial side of music was by no means neglected by the Germans. In Galveston, Sachtleben's Emporium of Music offered for sale all kinds of instruments and both domestic and imported sheet music. Music halls, often combined with turn-halls or dance-halls, were built to serve as meeting places and concert halls for the singing groups, whose numbers grew with the years. These buildings were rented to other organizations for various purposes.

The close relation of music and social life was particularly noticeable among the Germans. As in Germany, the beer gardens were the recreation centers to which the whole family repaired on Sundays and holidays. There the beer was sipped in leisurely fashion in a jovial atmosphere, while the band played and the groups sang. The children had the opportunity to hear music; the elders, an opportunity to create; and there can be small doubt that music did much to foster the feeling of good fellowship so characteristic of German neighborhoods. A good foundation was being laid, but, alas, the foundation

(41)

was nearly destroyed by the inroads of the Civil War. For almost ten years music had to give way to the sterner calls of life. Many Germans fled to Mexico to escape serving in the army; others were busy protecting the frontier and their homes against Indians. As both food and clothing were scarce, all efforts were turned toward satisfying these needs. Not until after the dark days of reconstruction were the Germans again able to devote their leisure hours seriously to music.

BOOK II

ABSORPTION FROM A
WIDER FIELD

CHAPTER VI

The Music of the Mexican War

FROM the time that secret orders were delivered to General Taylor in 1845 to proceed to Texas and there place his army in position for such action as circumstances might render advisable, the eyes of the world were turned to the Mexican border. Almost overnight the comparatively unsettled regions along the Rio Grande became the scene of feverish action. Troops and supply trains blazed trails through vast uninhabited stretches, and established camps in somnolent Mexican villages. Corpus Christi was the first of these to feel the effects of the increased activity, but all the settled portions of Texas were stirred by the arrival of large groups of men from various parts of the United States. New contacts, cultural as well as military, were quickly established. The martial spirit in the United States showed itself promptly through musical channels; publishers from Boston to New Orleans rushed patriotic music from their presses; new publications were rapidly forwarded to the front; and Texas, now for the first time the center of general interest, eagerly received and broadcasted the new music.

Some of this had Texas for its background. "Uncle Sam and Texas" was sung to the tune of *Yankee Doodle;* "Texas the Young Tree of Freedom," to that of *Harry Bluff;* "The Fair Land of Texas" to *When the Fair Land of Poland* while the "Flag of Texas", and "All for Texas" had original music. The evolution of Texas was commemorated through "The Alamo" by J. H. Hewitt; "Remember the Alamo" by T. A. Durriage, which was set to the tune of *Bruce's Address,* as was "The Texian General's Address to his Army" and "San Jacinto"; and "The Song of the Texas Ranger" sung to the tune of *I'm Afloat.*

As the war progressed, the various points in Mexico reached by the victorious army were quickly made familiar through songs and instrumental compositions. Corpus Christi and the

I'M AFLOAT! I'M AFLOAT!

ELIZA COOK

HENRY RUSSEL

I'm a-float! I'm a-float! on the fierce roll-ing tide, The o-cean's my home, and my bark is my bride! Up! up! with my flag! let it wave o'er the sea, I'm a-float! I'm a-float! and the ro-ver is free! I fear not the mon-arch, I heed not the law; I've a com-pass to steer by, a dag-ger to draw; And ne'er as a cow-ard or slave will 'I

kneel, While my guns car - ry shot, or my belt bears a steel! Quick!

quick! trim her sails; let her sheets kiss the wind And I war - rant we'll

soon leave the sea - gulls be - hind; Up! up! with my flag! let it

wave o'er the sea! I'm a - float! I'm a - float! and the ro - ver is

free! I'm a - float! I'm a - float! and the ro - ver is free!

FIG. 21

This music was well known in Texas as "The Ranger's Song" with
the following text:

(47)

Mount, mount, and away o'er the green pastures wide,
The sword is our scepter, the fleet steed our pride.
Up, up with our flag, let its bright star gleam out!
Mount, mount and away on the wild border scout.

We care not for danger, we heed not the foe,
Where our brave steeds can bear us, right onward we go;
And never, as cowards, can we fly from the fight
While our belts hold a blade, our star sheds its bright light.

Then mount and away! give the fleet steed the rein,
The Ranger's at home on the prairie again;
Spur, spur in the chase, dash on to the fight,
Cry vengeance for Texas and God speed the right.

The might of the foe gathers thick in our way,
They hear our wild shout as we rush to the fray;
What to us is the fear of the death-stricken plain,
We have "braved it before, and will brave it again."

The death-dealing bullets around us may fall,
They may strike, they may kill, but they cannot appal;
Through the red field of carnage right onward we'll wade,
While our guns carry ball, and our hands wield the blade.

Hurrah, my brave boys! ye may fare as ye please,
No Mexican banner now floats in the breeze!
'Tis the flag of Columbia that waves o'er each height,
While on its proud folds our star sheds its light.

Then mount and away! give the fleet steed the rein,
The Ranger's at home on the prairie again;
Spur, spur in the chase, dash on to the fight,
Cry vengeance for Texas and God speed the right.

FIG. 22

Nueces had been abandoned in March, 1846, before publishers had fully awakened to the opportunity; but by the time the Rio Grande was reached by Taylor's force, composers were adding fame both to individuals and places. "General Taylor's Grand March" by Grobe; "General Taylor's Quickstep;" "Rough and Ready" by F. A. Durivage; "Rough and Ready" by Austin Phillips; "Zachary Taylor;" "Hurrah for Rough and Ready," which begins "Strike for our Right" and is set to the tune of *Rose of Alabama,* are but a few of the musical compositions quickly made familiar in Texas.

The arrival of the troops at the Rio Grande was celebrated in song and dance. "The Rio Grande;" "The Rio Bravo, a Mexican Lament" by Austin Phillips; "The Fort Brown Quickstep" by Getze; "The Point Isabel Chaunt"; "The Coast of Mexico," sung to the tune of *Lucy Neal;* "We're the Boys for

Mexico;" "Wave, Wave the Banner High," sung to the melody of *March to the Battle Field;* "The American Bivouac on the Banks of the Rio Grande;" and "Capt. Walker's Quickstep" by Grobe, honoring the leader of the Texas Rangers, were among the many. "On to the Charge" by Hewitt and a "Funeral March" by Mattias Kellar were written in memory of Ringgold, who fell at Fort Brown; "Fire Away," set to the tune *The Campbells are Coming,* was the song of Ringgold's

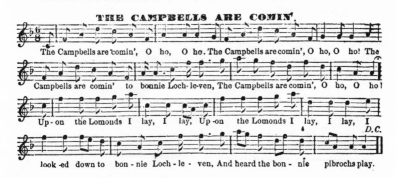

THE CAMPBELLS ARE COMIN'.

The Campbells are 'comin', O ho, O ho. The Campbells are comin', O ho, O ho! The Campbells are comin' to bonnie Loch-le-ven, The Campbells are comin', O ho, O ho! Up-on the Lomonds I lay, I lay, Up-on the Lomonds I lay, I lay, I look-ed down to bon-nie Loch-le-ven, And heard the bon-nie pibrochs play.

D.C.

FIG. 23

artillerists. There was also a "Funeral March" dedicated to Colonel Watson; and "Watson's Lament," with words by W. K. Dean, was published in Baltimore.

The occupation in May of the first Mexican town beyond the Rio Grande called forth a new wave of musical enthusiasm. "The Fall of Matamoros," "The Matamoros Grand Triumphal March and Quickstep;" and the "Matamoros Grand March" commemorated this event. "Palo Alto, or Our Army on the Rio Grande," given in New Orleans in November, 1846; the "Palo Alto Grand March;" and "Palo Alto and Resaca de la Palma" by Prevost—the first music engraved on zinc in New Orleans; "Palo Alto," a song beginning "Now while our cups are flowing;" "Le Capt. May et le General de la Vega sur les bords du Rio Grande"—a one-act comic opera, the libretto by Felix de Coermont and music by Fourmestroux; and "Here's a Health to Thee, May" are a few of the vocal productions that marked the advance inland.

Buena Vista was the subject of six songs: "On Buena Vista's Bloody Field" by Col. Henry Petrunken; "Buena Vista," beginning "Near Buena Vista's Mountain Chain;" another by the same title, beginning "From the Rio Grande's waters to the icy lakes of Maine," by Albert Pike; "The Dead at Buena Vista," words by Thos. G. Spear, on hearing of the fall of Henry Clay, Jr., and sung to the tune of *Burial of Sir John Moore*; "A Song of Buena Vista" by Alison Phillips; and "The Battle of Buena Vista" with words by John G. Dunn. Among the marches were "The Buena Vista Grand March;" "Buena Vista," dedicated to Gen. Woll; and "General Taylor's March at Buena Vista," by Reimer. An opera by that title was composed by Prevost and performed in New Orleans before May 24, 1847.

Most popular of subjects from September, 1846, for over a year while the army was pushing forward from Vera Cruz to the City of Mexico, was Monterey. "The storming of Monterey" by F. Buck and "The Monterey Grand Waltz" were among the instrumental compositions. Songs were more numerous: "The Storming of Monterey," words by Gardenier; "Monterey," dedicated to Gen. Taylor; "Monterey, a National Song;" another "Monterey, a National Song" with words by Watson and music by Austin Phillips; "The Fields of Mexico or the American Maiden's Song to her Lover," which begins "Wouldst thou have me leave thee, dearest"; "The Field of Monterey" by Sullivan; "Monterey" by Bayard Taylor, which begins "We were not many, we who stood"; and "The Soldier's Widow," which ends with the line "Than he who fell at bloody Monterey." Especially famous was the incident of the Mexican girl killed while extending aid to injured United States soldiers; this called forth novels, poems, and the songs "The Heroine of Monterey" and "The Maid of Monterrey" by John H. Hewitt. This became one of the most famous songs of the war; the tune was sung in Texas with the original words for over half a century, and later adapted to various other texts including that of the gospel hymn "I want to be an Angel."

The storming and capture of Vera Cruz in March, 1847, served as new inspiration for instrumental compositions, among which were "The Fall of Vera Cruz" by Francis Buck; "The Vera Cruz Quickstep" by E. Wathan; "The Vera Cruz Grand

THE MAID OF MONTEREY

Words and Music
By John H. Hewitt

1. The moon was shin-ing bright-ly Up - on the bat-tle plain; The
2. She cast a look of an - guish On dy - ing and on dead, Her
3. She gave the thirst-y wa - ter, And dress'd the bleed-ing wound; And
4. For, tho' she loved her na - tion And prayed that it might live, Yet,

gen - tle breeze fann'd light - ly The fea - tures of the slain; The
lap she made the pil - low Of those who groan'd and bled. And
gen - tle prayers she ut - ter'd For those who sigh'd a - round. And
for the dy - ing foe - men She had a tear to give. Then,

guns had hush'd their thun - der, The drum in si - lence lay; When
when the dy - ing sol - dier For one bright gleam did pray, He
when the bu - gle sound - ed Just at the break of day; We
here's to that bright beau - ty Who drove death's pang a - way, The

came the Se - ño - ri - ta, The maid of Mon - te - rey; The
bless'd the Se - ño - ri - ta, The maid of Mon - te - rey; And
bless'd the Se - ño - ri - ta, The maid of Mon - te - rey; And
meek - eyed Se - ño - ri - ta, The maid of Mon - te - rey; Then,

guns had hush'd their thun - der, The drum in si - lence lay, When
when the dy - ing sol - dier For one bright gleam did pray, He
when the bu - gle sound - ed Just at the break of day, We
here's to that bright beau - ty Who drove death's pang a - way, The

came the Se - ño - ri - ta, The maid of Mon - te - rey.
bless'd the Se - ño - ri - ta, The maid of Mon - te - rey.
bless'd the Se - ño - ri - ta, The maid of Mon - te - rey.
meek - eyed Se - ño - ri - ta, The maid of Mon - te - rey.

FIG. 24

(51)

March" by Chadwick; and the "Grand Military Quadrille." "Cerro Gordo Grand March and Quickstep by a Texan Youth" is evidence that Texas was contributing.

The arrival of the army at the capital was also chronicled in song. "The Men of Churubusco" was set to music from *Norma;* and "Hurrah for the Halls of Montezuma" was sung to the overworked melody of *Yankee Doodle.*

All of this music reached Texas in some form, and much of it became a part of that passed down to succeeding generations. It was through this music that Texas was first brought into close touch with the wider world of music; and through the various songs and instrumental compositions linked with Texas localities, events, and people, the outside world was introduced to, and became familiar with, the new state.

FIRE AWAY!

The Song of Ringgold's Artillerists

Tune—"The Campbells are Coming"

The Mexican bandits
  Have crossed to our shore;
Our soil has been dyed
  With our countrymen's gore.
The murderer's triumph,
  Was theirs for a day—
Our triumph is coming—
  So fire—fire away!

Be steady—be steady—
  And firm every hand—
Pour your shot like a storm
  On the murderous band.
On their flanks, on their center,
  Our batteries play—
And we sweep them like chaff,
  As we fire—fire away!

'Tis over—the thunders
  Have died on the gale—
Of the wounded and vanquished
  Hark! hark to the wail!
Long the foreign invader
  Shall morn for the day,
When Ringgold was summoned
  To fire—fire away!

CHAPTER VII

Other Foreign Contributors

EVEN before the Anglo-Americans and Germans came into Texas in large numbers, other nationalities had begun to contribute in a lesser degree to musical life in Texas. During the 18th century the eastern neighbor of the Texans had been the French in Louisiana, and the contacts became much closer after 1762 when Louisiana was ceded to Spain. From that time until the territory was sold to the United States in 1803, there was a constant intermingling of the two peoples both socially and commercially—an intermingling which left its impress upon various aspects of the culture of both—especially upon the music.

Any reference to the music of the French in the Southwest brings in the term "creole," a word often misunderstsood. A creole is a child of European parents born in America; the pure-blooded descendants of French and Spanish settlers in America are the real creoles, although the term, by popular usage, has been applied to the offspring of mixed marriages, regardless of color. The latter element enters largely into the general application of the term in Louisiana, for there the negro population was large, through the contant influx from the West Indies. Out of the mixture of French, Spanish and negro life grew the music of today known as "creole." Which blood was the greatest contributor has been disputed. "The melancholy, quavering beauty and weirdness of the negro chant are lightened by the French influence or subdued and deepened by the Spanish," wrote Lafcadio Hearn. Krebhiel admits that the basic rhythm of the negro was that of the "Habanera," but he credits the Spaniards with having borrowed it from the negroes.

Regardless of the origin of the rhythms and melodies, there was in Louisiana a mass of folk music among the people. Since the French were fond of dancing, many of the French folk and and court dances of the 18th century were known in New Orleans. The Acadians, those unfortunate peasants made famous by *Evangeline,* are credited with having introduced many songs; of the people scattered along the Gulf Coast, the small group settled near Port Arthur is of special interest to Texas. These "cajuns" as they came to be called, in trying to make new homes on the Texas coast, had little in the way of solace but their simple songs. They lived to themselves; even after Texas was predominantly Anglo-American, descendants of these people remained aloof, clung to their own language and customs, and kept alive what semblances of culture their ancestors had known. Some of their songs are still to be heard, in more or less corrupted forms, along the Texas coast and in the "cajun" district extending into Louisiana. One of these is "Va ingrate bergere."

It was during the period of Spanish occupancy that a most important forward step in the cultivation of music was taken in New Orleans, and its reflection was heard in Texas. In 1791, following an insurrection in Santo Domingo, an opera company took refuge in New Orleans and was heartily received by both the French and Spanish populace. To house them an opera house was built, and from that time on companies of singers and players, often brought to America under subsidies of the Spanish government at Havana or Mexico, stopped at New Orleans. Opera had been common in both Mexico and Havana since before 1700 and no doubt many of the songs later heard in mangled forms of French or Spanish from the lips of the negroes were brought to the Crescent City by European singers.

From New Orleans both French and Spanish music was carried into Texas and New Mexico by traders, enterprising investigators, and their followers, who, despite restrictions, were constantly lured westward. Especially strong was the tide of French-Spanish immigration after the announcement of the purchase of Louisiana by the United States, many claiming they were unwilling to live under the new government. Various types of creole songs became known in the Spanish border province; those dedicated to the black-eyed señoritas were in strong evidence; but songs, under cover of which remarks and illusions not otherwise permissible were included, are to be found among the official records of Texas. Before and after Texas became independent there was a slight infiltration of French music from the several colonies of French and Swiss who located at various points. In 1817 a group of exiles settled on the Trinity; but they soon scattered.

Various Frenchmen drifted into Texas after 1821 and some brought their families and made permanent homes in the region, but it was not until 1844 that another distinctly French colony, Castroville, was established on the Medina River, some twenty miles west of San Antonio, by Henry Castro who brought over several hundred families. We get glimpses of the cultural life of the group from Emanuel Domenech, who served the community as parish priest during some years. Among the songs he mentions in connection with Texas was:

> Oh, surtout cache-lui
> D'ou vient non ennui,

which he heard in San Antonio, and

> Vogue, vogue, oh ma balancelle,

a boat song he himself sang on the Medina River. After two years in the wilds, as he termed the region, this French priest returned to France and wrote his impressions of Texas.

Even before Domenech issued his volume descriptive of the new state of the American Union, others were turning their eyes in its direction. In 1854 Victor Considerant, a French economist who believed in the socialistic principle of work alike and share alike, persuaded a group of French and Swiss, who were dissatisfied with conditions at home, to emigrate to Texas and establish there a colony in which there would be complete freedom and independence. In this group of five hundred were some highly educated people, artists, writers, and musicians; in the latter group were Mrs. Vigoreaux, the mother-in-law of the founder, Charles Capys, and Allyre Bureau, who had been the musical director of the Odeon, a Paris theater. After landing on the Texas coast, they travelled with many difficulties to the vicinity of Dallas, where, near the present suburb of Oak Cliff, they established "La Reunion," on land Considerant had previously purchased. But homes had to be built, and crops planted and harvested in order that all might live. Those of the group unaccustomed to manual labor found life in Texas very different from what they dreamed. The

(55)

CLANG! CLANG! CLANG!

Abbie Farwell Brown
From the French.

Allyre Bureau

From the *Progressive Music Series*. Used by permission of Silver Burdett and Co.

Fig. 25
(56)

heat of the Texas sun through the long hot summer was scorching to people accustomed to Alpine regions; and the Texas northers swept down upon them before adequate housing could be providied. They planted wheat only to have it eaten up by grasshoppers.

Utterly unprepared for the conditions they were to meet,

CHOOSING A FLOWER

Miriam Clark Potter
From the French.

Allyre Bureau

Allegretto

1. "Come flow-ers to me! I'll choose one, the fair - est, The fin - est, the rar - est, My sis - ter to be." "The tu - lip is gay - est, Most gor-geous-ly drest; And loved by the sun - light A - bove all the rest."

2. "Too haugh - ty is she; Of flow - ers, the proud - est, In col - ors, the loud - est; She'll not do for me". "The vio - let is mod - est, And fair - est of face; She loves the deep for - est With beau - ty to grace."

3. "But she is too shy; She shuns the bright mea dows, And hides in the shad - ows Her big gol - den eye." "The rose smiles up - on you From beau - ti - ful bow'rs; Choose her for your sis - ter, The queen of all flow'rs."

4. "Though love - ly the rose, Her play-mates she teas - es With thorns when she pleas - es, As ev - 'ry - one knows". "No flow - er is per - fect, No mat - ter how rare; Come, play with us all then, Thro' sum - mer days fair."

From the *Progressive Music Series.* Used by permission of Silver Burdett and Co.

FIG. 26

(57)

these pioneers had brought with them a piano, an organ. flutes and violins; these indeed proved a means of recreation. In the community house, the whole group met once or twice a week for singing. Here Allyre Bureau composed some songs which his compatriots sang—among these "Clang, Clang, Clang," and "Choosing a Flower," included later in the *Progressive Music Series* and still sung delightedly today by our school children.

But before long many were dissatisfied; the leader Considerant and a group of the colonists moved to San Antonio, and later returned to France. Of those who stayed in Texas, some became prominent citizens of Dallas, one later served as mayor; others moved to San Antonio and contributed in some degree to the development of musical life in that city. Bureau set out with a small group who intended to sail for France, but he died before he reached the coast and is buried in Texas soil, near Houston.

The Czech immigrants, a few of whom began to drift in during the thirties, became a much more numerous group with the passing of time. During the fifties many arrived; at this time Fayetteville, Dubina, Praha, and Hostyn were settled. Among the newcomers were physicians, lawyers, bankers, educators, and musicians. Others continued to come until, in the fifty-four Czech settlements in the state, there are in 1936 some 300,000 Czechs. Musical organizations were early established; bands formed; and good music maintained in the churches. Czecho-Slovakia, or Bohemia, is especially rich in folk-songs; it is especially these that have lived in Texas. The Czech folk-songs and folk-dances are popularized today by numerous musical organizations which devote themselves specifically to the cultivation of the music of their fatherland.

Of the other nationalities who made settlements in Texas before the Civil War the Swedes were the most important. The leader was Sir Swante Palm, for many years the Swedish consul at Austin. This scholarly gentleman and good musician, who served as the first organist of the Swedish Lutheran church of the capital, did much to encourage musical activities among his countrymen, many of whom he had been instrumental in bringing to Texas. Near Austin, at New Sweden and at Round Rock, Swedish groups settled; in each community was

COME! O COME WITH ME

light and free! To ply the feather'd oar Is joy to me; And while we glide a-

moon is beam_ing; Come, oh!come with me the stars are gleaming All a_round,a_

_long, my song shall be: "My dear___est maid I love but thee."

_bove, with beau__ty teem__ing: Moonlight hours are meet for-love.

Fine.

FIG. 27

a church which conducted its services in Swedish, and at Round
Rock and Austin Swedish colleges were established and maintained throug many years. The church choirs specialized in
the beautiful Swedish *chorales.* At midsummer, a festival was
held at which singers from the various choirs were combined
into a large chorus, which sang music of a high type. Folk
and art songs of Sweden and Germany were thus kept alive
and made familiar to the younger generation. At the Lutheran
Encampment, an annual affair, the combined choirs frequently
rendered choral works of a high type. Sir Swante Palm gathered about him an extensive Swedish library, a large part of
which he left at his death to the University of Texas. Among
the books he bequeathed to the Swedish Lutheran Church at
Austin are many volumes of Swedish music, representative of
the best of his day.

One of the later foreign settlers; the Italians, many of whom
established themselves near Del Rio and Bryan, introduced
many simple but lovely melodies. One early known in Texas
is "Come, oh Come With Me."

CHAPTER VIII

Echoes From The Old South

IN spite of the presence within her borders before 1860 of
many foreign elements and of large groups of settlers from
northern states of the Union, Texas was at heart a part of
the Old South, as was clearly demonstrated by the Act of Se-
cession, passed early in 1861. The culture and tradition of
the dominant class had largely been transplanted westward
along the Gulf Coast; and the political philosophy of the South
was destined to determine the course Texas followed as a
state.

While the privations and suffering of many of the other
southern states during the Civil War were never known within
the boundaries of Texas, because only part of her territory fell
into Union hands and her proximity to Mexico made possible
the uninterrupted exportation of cotton and the importation
of not only necessities but even some luxuries, her people
shared the mental anguish of those years. Little by little the
state was depleted of its man force; they went to the front either
voluntarily or by coercion, or else they sought refuge in Mexico to avoid conscription—a procedure followed by many of
the foreign element which as a whole was hostile to slavery.
As a result the singing societies, the bands, and the orchestras,
entirely male organizations in those days, were soon disbanded,
not to resume their activities until after the close of the war.

From the press it has been possible to cull bits which give
some insight into musical life during those years. During 1861
came an influx of patriotic music from the presses of New Orleans, Richmond, and Augusta as well as Galveston, which
issued early in the year "The Southern Pleiades" (7 stars),
a march and quickstep by Edward C. Wharton, published by
August Sachtleben. Among the songs were Macarthy's
"The Bonny Blue Flag," "Missouri," and "The Volunteers;"
Blackmar's "The Southron's Chaunt of Defiance;" Stanton's
"Dixie War Song;" Alice Lane's "Stars of our Banner;"

George's "The Confederate Flag;" Glover's "The Southron's Watchword;" and "God will Defend the Right" by a lady of Richmond. "The Beauregard Manassas Quickstep" and "Beauregard's Grand March" were among the instrumental compositions. The importation of pianos into Galveston kept pace with the diversity of sheet music, and a serenading band was organized there by Charles Hoffman, evidently with the expectation that the war would be speedily over.

With the beginning of 1862 music came into service for benefit purposes. Concerts were given in the various cities for the benefit of families of soldiers. In Galveston the Confederate Minstrels made their appearance, and concerts provided revenue for the support of Dr. Bryan's Hospital and assistance for the rangers. Among new patriotic songs was "The Southern Marseillaise." The sentimental included "Carrie Bell" and "I would Like to Change my Name" by La Hache; "Violette" by Eaton; reprintings of foreign songs such as Kucken's "We Met by Chance" and "How can I Leave Thee;" Mengis' "Switzer's Farewell;" Abt's "When the Swallows Homeward Fly;" and old Scotch songs like "Annie Laurie," "Mary of Argyle" and "Bonnie Jean." "The Confederates Grand March" by Hartwell appeared in its fourth edition during that year.

With the opening of 1863 the seriousness of the situation was generally felt. Despite the more marked exodus of troops, music continued. Concerts were given in Houston for the benefit of both Hood's and Sibley's brigades and for the Terry Rangers; another contributed to the hospital fund. Professor Frenel composed a new march in honor of General Magruder. Concerts and tableaux in Rutersville provided further funds for the Rangers; Hallettsville raised over four hundred dollars for Young's regiment. Among the other concerts in Houston was a program of orchestral music by Charles Otis; one in April for Baylor's Brigade; in May for the General Hospital; in June there were juvenile concerts; in October, an amateur program for the Davis Guards; and in November the Star State Minstrels gave a benefit for the Soldier's Home. The establishment of a musical academy in Houston during the fall suggests that musical education was still being earnestly promoted.

With Galveston, as well as New Orleans, in Federal hands
there was small chance for such merchandise as new music to
enter Texas. Indeed the publication in the South had been
more and more limited until Blackmar in Augusta was almost
the only house left which continued to issue sheet music. John
H. Hewitt, whose songs were widely popular, maintained a
music business there until 1863, when he, too, saw the future.
and returned to Baltimore. Of the songs published during that
year which found their way sooner or later into Texas were
Hewitt's "The South;" Anna Ford's "The Prisoner's Lament;"
Ilsley's "The Drummer Boy of Shiloh;" Mayer's "Keep the
Powder Dry;" and one edition of "Maryland, My Maryland,"
with the music attributed to a lady of Baltimore. One publication from the house of George Dunn at Richmond entitled
Christmas and New Year Musical Souvenir was made up of
three songs: "Fairies Have Broken Their Wings," with words
by Thomas Hood; "The Lover's Wish," text by Rosier; and
"I Know a Maiden Fair to See" by Longfellow, all set to
music by "F. W. R."

The year 1864 saw music in Texas at low ebb. A concert
by Madame Rheinhardt, a pupil of Mendelssohn, and the
benefit concerts, especially for the destitute soldiers and their
families, were the ouly items of interest. In New Braunfels five
of these followed each other in rapid succession. With 1865
the sky began to clear. Madame Bishop visited Texas and by
the middle of the year male teachers began to insert their ad-
vertisements in the local press, Charles Otis in Houston and F.
W. Smith in La Grange being among the first. In October.
Miss Mollie Moore, later known as a gifted poetess, appeared
as a pianist, and in that same month musical items, including
one on Franz Listz, began to appear in the Houston *Telegraph*.
Concerts for benefit purposes continued, one for General Hood
being sponsored in San Antonio by Professors Plagge and
Heilig. The United States army bands stationed at such posts
as San Antonio gave frequent concerts.

Aside from that group of songs that typified the last flare
of patriotic spirit before the end of the struggle, such as "There's
Life in the Old Land Yet;" Macarthy's "Origin of the Stars
and Bars;" and Mordaunt's "Brave Boys are They," many
others appeared. These were principally love songs or songs

(63)

LORENA

H. D. L. Webster

J. P. Webster

The years creep slowly by, Lorena,
    The snow is on the grass again;
The sun's low down the sky, Lorena,
    The frost gleams where the flow'rs have been;
But the heart throbs on as warmly now,
    As when the summer days were nigh;
Oh! the sun can never dip so low,
    Adown af'fection's cloudless sky,
The sun can never dip so low,
    Adown af'fection's cloudless sky,

A hundred months have passed Lorena,
    Since last I held that hand in mine;
And felt the pulse beat fast Lorena,
    Though mine beat faster far, than thine:
A hundred months have passed, Lorena
    When up the hilly slope we climbed,
To watch the dying of the day,
    And hear the distant church bells chime,
To watch the dying of the day,
    And hear the distant church bells chime,

FIG. 28

---

of home. Of the latter type were "What is Home Without Mother?" "Childhood Hours are Fleeting By" by Eaton; "Let Me Kiss Him for His Mother" by Ordway; "Take Me Home to the Place;" and "Listen to the Mocking Bird." Among the love songs sung through the years which always awaken recollections of the life of the Old South were "Bonnie Eloise," "Angel of Dreams" by Eaton; Webster's "Lorena" and the reply to it; Stephen Foster's "I See Her Still in My Dreams;" Daly's "Dying Camille;" Bucklet's "I am Dreaming Still of Thee;" "I'm Leaving Thee in Sorrow, Annie;" and "Juanita." Of the songs popular in those days, only "Nellie Gray" is suggestive of slave life.

The evolution of a song in Texas is well illustrated in the case of "Take Me Home to the Place Where I First Saw the Light." In its original form it bore no relation to the South; it was a transplanted flower when first known in Texas. Sung through many years in this form, it was borrowed for camp meeting, and became known as "At the Cross," widely used later as a gospel hymn. During the trail-driving years, when the cattle industry made the cowboy a feature of Texas life,

(65)

this song was paraphased in the cow-camp, with the following result:

At the bar, at the bar
Where I smoked my first cigar,
And my nickels and my dimes rolled away;
It was there by chance
That I tore my Sunday pants,
And now I can wear them every day.

TAKE ME HOME

FIG. 29

Take me home to the place where I first saw the light,
To the sweet sunny South take me home,
Where the mocking bird sung me to rest ev'ry night,
Ah! why was I tempted to roam,
I think with regret of the dear ones I left,
Of the warm house that sheltered me then,
Of the wife and the dear ones of whom I'm bereft,
And I sigh for the old place again.

(67)

CHORUS

Take me home to the place where my little ones sleep,
Poor massa lies buried close by
O'er the grave of the lov'd ones I long to weep,
And among them to rest when I die.

Take me home to the place where the orange trees grow,
To my cot in the evergreen shade,
Where the flowers on the river's green margin may blow,
Their sweets on the bank where we played,
The path to our cottage they say has grown green,
And the place is quite lonely around;
And I know that the smiles and the forms I have seen,
Now lie deep in the dark mossy ground.

Take me home, let me see what is left that I know—
Can it be that the old house is gone!
The dear friends of my childhood indeed must be few,
And I must lament all alone.
But yet I'll return to the place of my birth,
Where my children have played at the door;
Where they pull'd the white blossoms that garnish'd the
    earth,
Which will echo their footsteps no more.

CHAPTER IX

Some Musical Annals of Texas Before 1890

MUSICAL development following the Civil War varied with the different social classes. In general there were five classes of people: (1) the well-to-do whites, who having depended entirely upon slaves for labor, were accustomed to leisure which was devoted either to recreation or to the cultivation of the arts; (2) the poor whites, who earned only a pittance by manual labor, were socially almost on a par with the negroes, and knew no music except the songs they had heard in the regions from which they had come—largely hymn tunes or English, Irish, and Scotch folk-songs; (3) the foreigners, of whom the Germans were the most numerous, who having always done their own work, were entirely unaffected by the freeing of the slaves; (4) the Mexicans, mainly in San Antonio and the border regions, music loving but not active or enterprising promoters; and (5) the negroes, instinctively music lovers, but now faced for the first time with the problem of self-support. Staggered by the outcome of the war, the members of the ex-slave-holding class were far more than a decade in becoming adjusted to the changed conditions; the poor whites, like the negroes, were just beginning to emerge from a state of bondage. Under such conditions the development of music fell mainly to the foreign population, and it was only in the centers that boasted a substantial German population that any noteworthy musical progress was made. The sale of musical instruments in all parts of the state in the post war years was extensive.

Among the more important centers were Houston, Galveston, San Antonio, Austin, and the smaller German settlements headed by New Braunfels. Houston and Galveston, through their direct contact with New Orleans, Mexico and Europe, were visited frequently by foreign musicians; in San Antonio were both the German and Mexican elements; Austin, the capital, and the home of a large German group, was also a leader musically. In all these towns, the musical organizations formed before the war began to function again shortly after, under new leaders; concerts were frequent, and the study of music under private teachers was given encouragement.

Both the type of music studied and performed indicated a great advance musically over that of the earlier decade. Particularly was this noticeable among the Anglo-Americans, who formerly had contented themselves largely with the popular music of the day.

Some of the incidents in the musical life of these towns are of interest. Houston, enjoying the advantages of its proximity to the sea coast and its position as an early railroad center, was quickly able to return to normal conditions. Soon after the German Glee Club was reorganized and, under the leadership of Professor Miller assisted by Professor Eckhardt and C. G. Heine, gave a series of vocal and instrumental concerts, some of which were for charitable purposes, such as the support of the Bayland Orphan Home and to assist worthy negroes.

By 1868 the Houston theater was again in operation, and there Professor Stadtler, who had already organized a string and brass band, as well as various singing societies, directed the music. Even in the saloons of that day the music must have been rather superior to that later, for we find Professor Stadtler and his band, when not engaged in the theater, busy with evening concerts at the Exchange saloon.

The outstanding events in the musical life of Houston during the first decade after the Civil War were the Volkfests of 1869 and 1870. There was competitive singing by groups from Houston and Galveston, and programs which included works of Beethoven and Schubert were well rendered. When news of the Franco-Prussian War was received, benefit concerts for the German widows and orphans were given. Two excellent bands under the direction of Messrs. Schmidt and Stadtler gave public concerts and took part in all civic celebrations.

Music teaching went on apace. Private teachers taught in the schools and at their own and the pupils' home. In 1868 the *Houston Telegram* announced the "starting of a new enterprise in musical education"—that of teaching music in classes. "The plan is meeting with marked success in Europe and elsewhere." Mr. A. Adey, who introduced the plan in Houston, opened in that year the Houston Conservatory of Music, which offered a complete musical education including class lessons and concerts.

Among the other contributions to the musical life of Houston in the early seventies were the concerts given in 1873 by Eusebio Delgado, a well-known violinist of Mexico City, and by the Peak bellringers and the Berger family, vocalists, harpists, and violinists. For those of less cultivated tastes, the burlesque opera troupes, presented with the brass bands of the various minstrel shows which visited the city, offered entertainment.

Galveston, from the early days of the Republic, gave promise of becoming a musical center, for her location as a port was such that most of the newcomers, including musicians from either New York, Mobile, New Orleans, or Europe, landed there, and it also became the headquarters of the state for musical supplies. Pianos of the best manufacture, such as Wm. Hall, Chickering, Gilbert and Haines, were on sale regularly after 1850. Other instruments, especially violins, guitars, flutes, accordions, and tamborines, were regularly kept in stock and rarer instruments offered from time to time. Piano tuners from Galveston were sent to all parts of the state on annual or semi-annual trips. Sheet music and music books in a large and varied assortment were regularly advertised by Galveston merchants from the early fifties. Just after the Civil War the house of Thomas Goggan was established, which, with its branches, has served a wide circle of musicians and has published compositions of both Texans and Mexicans. Even before the establishment of Goggan's, music written by local musicians was being published in Galveston. One of these, of which a copy has survived, was "Leaf by Leaf the Roses Fall" by T. B. Bishop. A few of Mr. Fitze's compositions were also published there, but many were issued by Oliver Ditson. Another early composer was F. Smith, who taught at Baylor University. His "Holly Oak Grand Waltz" was one of the early compositions which had its origin in Texas and was published by a reputable house. Attention has already been called to Civil War Compositions.

Theater and concert life in Galveston had reached a point during the fifties that justified the erection of the Tremont Music Hall, which was owned and operated by August Sachtleben. The organization of several German singing societies as well as the Turn verein had taken place much earlier. Aside from the music furnished by local talent, the list of visiting artists who appeared in Galveston before the Civil War included many celebrities, some of these foreigners, such as Anna Bishop, the Bernais Mountain Singers, and the Hungarian exiles. An interesting figure connected with Galveston musical life in the fifties was Adah Isaacs Menken, a world-famed dancer and singer, who married Mr. Menken, a Galveston musician, in that city in 1856.

The Civil War put an end to all musical activities, for, due to the capture of the city by the Federals, the inhabitants fled to the mainland. The loss of the files of the *Galveston News* during this period has robbed the historian of much valuable material concerning Galveston in two decades. But scarcely was the war over before such organizations as the Harmonic Society, the Liedertafel, Liederkranz, St. Cecilia Brass Band, Lone Star Brass Band, a colored brass band, the Mozartina and the Island City Glee Clubs and the Philharmonic Society were all functioning.

In the churches Galveston was early blessed with unusually good music given under the direction of capable organists and choir directors. The Cathedral at Galveston boasted the first pipe organ in Texas. It was contracted for at a cost of $2,000, by Bishop Odin, and installed by Professor Felton, whose children all became accomplished musicians active in Galveston. Among the men who contributed later to the development of church music were Professors Sachtleben, Zawadil and Leberman, one of whose sons became a music teacher at the State school for the Blind at Austin. For many years the father was organist and director of music at St. Mary's Cathedral, where a choir composed of excellent voices, including those of Miss Reybaud and Messrs. Waltersdorf and Walker, furnished a high type of music. As a compliment to Professor Leberman, the Mozartina and Island City Glee Clubs dedicated to him a performance in 1876.

San Antonio was musically very fortunate, for many of the cultured foreign settlers, driven back from the frontier by Indians and other hardships, took refuge there, and many representatives of the educated families of the Old South, in addition to the original Spanish and Mexican settlers made their permanent homes in that city. Even from New England had come families of considerable musical talent, such as the Tompkins group, consisting of a brother and two sisters, who early in the fifties journeyed to Texas, giving concerts on the way. The *Clarksville Standard*, in recording their first performance in Texas, spoke of them as singers of extraordinary musical talent and admired particularly their comic songs, although it admitted that the pathetic, especially the "Snow Storm" and the "Death of Ringgold" were beautifully sung. Mr. Tompkins taught in San Antonio for many years; one sister became Mrs. Enoch Jones, the other Mrs. Newton; all were prominent musically until their death; and some of their descendants have carried on their good work.

Other family groups very active in promoting musical life in the Alamo City through many decades were the Herffs and the LaCostes. The beautiful LaCoste voices are recalled still by the singing of the descendants of Ferdinand Herff and Zulema La Coste. Other active musicians of the seventies included Professor Plagge, for many years the superintendent of the public schools and for a time teacher of music in St. Mary's Hall, the Episcopal school for girls; Mr. Heilig, who began teaching music in the public schools in the early fifties; and Mr. Thielepape, the director of the Beethoven Club, who also served for a time as the mayor of the city. When Sidney Lanier, the southern poet, spent some time in San Antonio in the early seventies, he visited the Beethoven Club, played his flute for its members, and was enthusiastically received. His contacts with this group of singers furnished some of the most pleasurable incidents of his stay there.

One of the centers of musical life in San Antonio was the Casino, established before the Civil War and supported until the present day largely by the German element. Here concerts were almost a weekly occurrence. Operas were given with both singers and orchestra drawn from local talent; groups from the German singing societies were heard from time to time; and visiting musicians were given a cordial and appreciative welcome.

Music was generally provided for the public. Following the early Mexican custom, a city band played on the plaza once

a week or oftener; during the concerts the young men and women promenaded, while the elders occupied the seats about
the square. In addition to the city band, the military band
attached to the United States troops, stationed for a time
where the Gunter Hotel now stands, gave frequent concerts.
In the town was also an Italian harpist, Charley Calvello, who
directed a string band much in favor for dances and home
entertainments. Among the Mexicans a brass band, which
gave both outdoor and indoor concerts, was organized and
long maintained.

In the churches some good music was given. The Catholic churches—the Cathedral, St. Mary's and St. Joseph's—the
former catering especially to the Spanish, the latter to the German element of the community, maintained a high standard.
The first pipe organ in a Protestant church was that installed
in 1875 in St. Mark's Episcopal Church, which before that
time boasted only a melodeon. The other Protestant sects,
while encouraging hymn singing, did not exert themselves toward securing good musical instruments or trained choirs
until much later. In addition to the music on Sundays, some
concerts were given in the churches, largely by German or
German-American talent.

Children of most of the prosperous French and Spanish
families were generally sent away to school, frequently to
Europe; consequently the musical ranks were continually being
replenished by young people who had enjoyed opportunities
for hearing far more music than San Antonio could provide.
The activity of the Germans was largely directed to giving
their children a good education at home; in their educational
scheme music and gymnastics played an important part.

Just across from the present Gunter Hotel on Houston Street
stood Turner Hall, where the attention of both young and old
was directed to physical development and to the attainment
of some degree of vocal skill. Here also met for practice the
German singing societies, directed by trained musicians, who
instilled into their pupils, along with a general love of music
and a first-hand knowledge of many of the classics, the the realization of the necessity for serious work. Among the teachers
of the period in addition to Messrs. Plagg, Heilig and Thiele-

pape, were Mr. Petmecky, Mr. Clements, and Louis Eberhardt.

Various merchants handled musical instruments. Sweet and La Coste sold pianos and musical supplies; E. Pentrieder also carried such things in his varied stock. Judge Devine is generally ccredited with having the first piano; but even before the Civil War pianos were common in most of the homes; in the well-to-do German or Mexican residence, it was unusual not to have one. Guitars were very popular as accompaniments for solo and group singing, especially among the Mexicans, all of whom sang constantly the folk-songs of old Spain, while many of them played beautifully by ear.

In spite of the lack of transportation facilities, which made it difficult for musicians who visited other parts of the state to reach San Antonio, opera troupes from Mexico, and occasionally from Houston, came by stage and were always cordially greeted there by a large music-loving audience. It was in the years before the coming of the railroads that the foundations for the cosmopolitan and music-loving city, which San Antonio has since been acknowledged to be, were securely laid.

Among the musical organizations which came into existence in Austin, the capital, soon after the Civil War and worked for the benefit of the general public was a city string band, composed of eight of Austin's best musicians and directed by Henry A. Klotz, a musician who later taught at the State School for the Blind. A brass band was also organized among the Germans; these two united their forces in a concert in 1870 for the benefit of the widows and orphans of the Franco-Prussian War. The string band especially enjoyed popular favor and more than one concert was given to secure funds for its support. In 1872 George Herzog, who became the teacher of orchestra and organ at the Blind Institute, took charge of the brass band and later conducted an orchestra. In 1877 the Hicks City Band, composed of colored members, came into existence.

Through its organist and musical director, Mrs. Fanny L. Crooker, St. David's Episcopal church was active in fostering good music. Under her leadership a Philharmonic Society, which met semi-monthly for musical study, was organized, and soon undertook the serious study of oratorio. *Esther* was performed with fifteen soloists and a chorus of fifty; in 1875 the *Creation* was given by the same group with the cooperation of the other musicians in Austin. For fifteen years Mrs. Crooker played an important part in musical life in Austin; she was drowned in the Indianola flood in 1886. Soon after her death the church offered for sale the first pipe organ brought to Austin, an Aeolian Automatic, with eight sets of reeds, which had been installed about the time of Mrs. Crooker's arrival.

The center of musical life in Austin for more than twenty years was the Turner Hall which then faced on Colorado Street and was later converted into the Scottish Rite Cathedral. With a floor space forty-five by sixty-six feet and a stage thirty-five by forty-five feet, it was claimed to be the finest hall in the state. The Turn Verein early organized a Singing Society which in the early seventies was under the direction of L. Klappenbach. Later, the Saengerrunde came under the direction of William Besserer, who, after playing an important part in musical life in Austin for more than fifty years, died in 1931. Born in Austin in 1850 and educated in Germany, he returned to his native city early in the seventies and entered upon an active career. Few musical performances were staged without his aid; few were the musical organizations to which he did not at some time lend a helping hand. At Scholz' Garden, which became the property of the German Singing Society, the Austin Musical Union flourished for many years under his direction and gave opera and choral works of a high order. He also directed dramatic performances of the younger German set. In 1875 Schiller's birthday was celebrated with tableaux and incidental music; in 1876 *Prince Wolfgang of Anhalt* was given; in 1886 *Stradella* and Mendelssohn's *Lorelei* were performed by local talent under his direction.

The outstanding event of musical life in Austin during the seventies was the twelfth Saengerfest held there in April, 1879, to celebrate the twenty-fifth anniversary of the founding of the State Saengerbund. Delegations from San Antonio, New Braunfels, Dallas, Brenham, and Galveston joined with the

Austin Saegerrunde and a mixed chorus in a three-day session. Ten years later the city again welcomed the singers who took part in the seventeenth Saengerfest.

Numerous were the teachers and musicians who contributed to musical progress. Among those in the seventies were Udo Rhodius, pianist and composer; J. Messmer, who had played in concert with Paganini in London and Paris; C. T. Sisson, who composed much music popular in his day and acted as concert manager in Austin; and Mrs. Cecilia Townsend. In the eighties, Mrs. J. J. Lane, who taught at Hood's Seminary; Miss Virginia Latham, teacher of piano at the Blind Institute; Mr. and Mrs. Robbins at the Texas Female Institute; H. F. Gruendler who taught at the German and English Academy, and his wife at the Stewart Female Seminary where Miss Clara Revell also taught; Mrs. E. B. Harding at the Mendelssohn School of Music and Art; and Professor Besserer who taught in almost every school in the city at one time or another —all contributed to musical education. The first music teacher in connection with the public schools was Mrs. Bettie Tyler who taught in the "Graded School" in 1881-82.

During the decade many musical attractions visited Austin. Among them were the Carleton Opera Company, the Salisbury Troubadours, the Emma Abbott Opera Company, the Hungarian Gypsy Students, and minstrels galore. These with the band concerts, the operas, and other concerts by local talent gave an opportunity for the young people to hear and study good music, and for the older folk to take an active part both in its cultivation and enjoyment.

The beginnings of music in Dallas are to be found in the annals of that band of French, Belgian, and Swiss settlers who established in 1855, on a site only a few miles from Oak Cliff, the colony of "La Reunion" under the leadership of Victor Considerant. Among the individuals who figured most prominently in the musical life of the colony were: Mrs. Vigoreaux, the mother-in-law of Considerant, who taught for a number of years; Allyre Bureau, already mentioned; Abel Daelly, a flutist; and Charles Capys, the leader of a singing society.

The close of the Civil War found Dallas a struggling village of less than a thousand souls; but interest in music was not lacking. At an entertainment given to raise funds for the erection of the Methodist church in 1868, music was furnished by Dr. Willis and his class and by the Dallas Glee Club. Professor St. Clair gave lessons on the violin and flute and also taught dancing; Mrs. S. B. Halsell taught the piano and guitar. In that same year, instruments were ordered and a brass band organized under the leadership of Judson B. Steffee. This band, late in 1868, gave a concert at Lancaster in response to a request of the "Ladies Building Committee" and was assisted by Professor Steele's vocal class. Professor Steffee was a busy man, for he also organized and instructed the Mechanics Brass Band, formed that year at Waxahachie, a band in Lancaster, and a band at Weatherford. Mr. Kinney organized in Dallas a cornet band of eight members. Among other teachers who were active in the late sixties were Mrs. Ellen S. Smith and Professor J. D. Lackie, who taught both vocal and instrumental music and directed many concerts of local talent.

With the coming of another Swiss group in 1870, music was given additional impetus, for most of the newcomers, while artisans, were accustomed to turn to music as a regular form of diversion. As a result the Swiss Glee Club was organized and soon claimed an important place in social life. This with the Turner singing association, promoted music in many forms. A regular feature of Dallas life was the May Fest. at which songs in French and German usually featured the program. Concerts were frequently given by the Turner singing association, which was directed by Professor Bauer. a teacher and composer of standing. One of his compositions, a Christmas anthem, was performed at the Episcopal church in 1875, when almost all the good voices of the city took part under his direction. Another organization which traces its origin to the Swiss group was the Frohsinn, a singing society which took part in the Saengerfest at Austin in 1879 by singing "Wie hab ich dich geliebt" by Moehring; after that date, it appeared regularly on the Saegerfest programs.

As Dallas before the days of the railroads was further removed from contacts with visiting musical attractions than Galveston or San Antonio, its musicians were forced to depend more largely upon local talent and to develop it to a greater extent. That the programs given were not to be despised is evidenced by a survey of a few of the compositions rendered. In 1874 one opened with a piano duet of an operatic overture, the Infelice of *Ernani* was sung by Major Obenchain, and the Mad Scene of *Lucia de Lammermoor* by Miss Rivers; Mrs. Alice Fisher gave "Fleurs des Alpes," a Tyrolienne song, and the "Grand Air des Dragons de Villars"; while the program closed with Gottschalk's *Last Hope* played by Mr. W. G. Francis, who was rated as one of the best pianists in Dallas. A typical Turner concert was the following, given in 1875: Overture to *Tancredi*, Aria for tenor from *Der Freischutz*, Reichardt's *Das Bild der Rose* as chorus with tenor solo, selection from *Egmont* by the orchestra, a duet from *Martha*, and Kuntze's *Weingalopp* by the chorus under the direction of Theodore Bauer. Other musical organizations were the Concordia Club, organized in 1875, and the Cosmopolites, an amateur group which contributed minstrel performances. The Musicale Society, formed about the same time continued active for many years.

The banner year of Dallas musical life in the decades following the Civil War was 1883, in which the new opera house was opened and the state Saengerfest held its biennial festival there. For this occasion the Spanish Fort band of New Orleans was engaged at a cost of $6,000. The mixed chorus under Profesor Frees, numbering about seventy-five voices, prepared the *Rose Maiden* for presentation. Dallas proved no unworthy host to the delegations which arrived from Austin, San Antonio, Galveston, and Houston, as well as from many of the smaller cities, such as Terrell, Longview, Brenham, and Waco. Here was gathered, for the first time in the history of North Texas, a representative body of the best of Texas musicians, who rendered a program of which no region could feel other than pride.

CHAPTER X

Musical Education

SINCE the missions were the first schools in Texas, it might truthfully be said that music has had a place in the school curriculum since the days of the earliest settlements in the region; but it has not been included during the whole period since, nor has its progress been either steady or continuous. In the schools established under the civil government of Spain, no music was taught, nor do we find reference even to group singing. In the early Anglo-American schools, many of which taught both boys and girls, songs were generally sung, if the teacher was capable of singing; in the schools for girls, the guitar and piano were almost always among the branches of instruction offered for a special fee, which in the period before 1860 ranged around $20.00 per semester. There are few references to the teaching of other instruments; these were left largely to the private teachers, more or less capable, who, in large numbers, offered their services to the public from 1830 on.

The first specific instance of music taught in the public schools as a regular branch of the curriculum at public expense was at Galveston. Just when the subject was introduced is not clear, but in 1847 when a committee of citizens made a visitation of the schools they made the following report:

Music has been taught in all the schools, since their opening, by Mr. Hill, with that thoroughness and skill for which he is so well known in the city. The introduction of this beautiful art, as a branch of elementary education, has given universal satisfaction to all interested, and to none more entirely than the children themselves. This is no longer an experiment or a theory. Whether as a means of joyous recreation to the fagged and weary pupil, or as a weapon of discipline over the boisterous one, it is worth tenfold its cost; but when we contemplate its probable influence, as a moral hygiene, over the minds of our youth, at a season of life when impressions are the most lasting, its value is truly incalculable. Among the pupils there is a large number of Germans, many of whom entered the schools without knowing a word of English. These children now sing our National Airs correctly, and feelingly, and are forming their ideas of patriotism, and its duties, in their most pleasing association.

It is not difficult to explain the appearance of this branch of education at this comparatively early date. The movement toward inclusion of music as a regular branch of school instruction was in full swing. Efforts of school officials in Boston dating from 1830 finally secured the inclusion of music in 1838 in the public schools, with Lowell Mason as the teacher. During the next few years other cities rapidly fell in line:

Portland	1839	Buffalo	1843
New York	1840	Pittsburgh	1844
Cincinnati	1840	Salem	1844
New Orleans	1841	Providence	1844

Mr. Hill, the Galveston teacher, had come from New Orleans, where music had already been introduced in the schools of the Second Municipality.

Nor is it difficult to explain the interest in such a branch of study in a town as remote as Galveston from large cultural centers. Galveston was the port to which most of the Germans who were about to settle in Texas came. Many went no further; others lingered longer or shorter periods awaiting means of transportation to the new settlements inland. Accustomed as they were to music in their schools in the fatherland, it is small wonder that they lent their influence to its inclusion here. As the new German settlements were founded and schools established, music took its place in the curriculum. In San Antonio, Mr. Heilig became the teacher in "The People's Schools," as a receipt preserved at the City Hall testifies:

It is hereby agreed between Francis Heilig and the city of San Antonio through their school committee that said Heilig agrees to teach vocal music to the scholars of "The People's Schools" of San Antonio, by giving said scholars four lessons per week to be given at such hours as the teachers of the different schools may decide. For such service the city agrees to pay the said Heilig Ten Dollars per month, at the end of each month.

J. M. West

F. Heilig

J. Ulrich

Chairman of the School Committee

This agreement is dated 1853, and the records show that Mr. Heilig continued to perform that service for many years.

During the forties and fifties music was generally taught in the private institutions of learning, but this instruction generally covered no more than group singing for all, and piano or guitar

(81)

playing for the girls. Mrs. Seelfeld at Velasco, Miss Madden at Houston, the Misses Sims at Washington and Mrs. Mayo at Rutersville were among the early teachers. Wesleyan at San Augustine, the University of San Augustine, Nacogdoches University, and the Masonic Collegiate Institute at Fanthorpe, now Anderson, were among the schools that advertised this branch. Melinda Rankin recounts the presence of a good teacher of music at Matagorda for some years preceding 1850; and the Lavaca Institute offered instruction in both piano and guitar, as did the Boston Female Academy, where vocal music was made a part of each day's exercises. In 1851 Mr. L. H. W. Johnson was proposing to teach music by a system of mutual education and the use of figures:

> I would introduce to a class—say from seven years and upwards ---the science of music by figures, which from its combining pleasure with utility—its simplicity and facility of acquisiton—its moralizing and harmonizing influence is decidedly preferable to any other elementary branch for the purpose of attracting the attention, expanding the mind, and paving the way, or forming a prelude to other solid, scientific, ornamental, and useful branches of education. . .

In the following year Mr. G. G. Miner announced to the Houston public that he would instruct in both harmony and composition in addition to vocal and instrumental music. In 1853 Baylor Female College was advertising for a "thoroughly qualified" music teacher.

The Civil War was scarcely over before strong effort was made to include music as a part of the regular work of the public schools. At the meeting of the State Teachers Association in 1866, the standing committee on music, of which H. Ernest Vaas and Gustave Duvernoy, both of Houston, were members, reported on the adoption of a text book in music, *The Silver Lute* by Geo. F. Root, published in Cincinnati by John Church and Co. in 1862. Extant copies point to its wide popularity, both in the day and Sunday schools. Of the various state superintendents who urged the teaching of music, Prof. Hollingsworth was a leader. The *Acme Song Collection* recommended by him is the first textbook seen by the writer which contains songs with a specific reference to Texas, one being an adaption of *Dixie* to words descriptive of Texas conditions. The company which issued it also circulated small prospectuses which contained printed music; and even these seem to have come into popular use.

HURRAH! THE GRAND YOUNG STATE OF TEXAS

Oh! our Texan State is a grand creation,
The largest of all this glorious nation.
Then hurrah! hurrah! hurrah! sing we all.

CHORUS: The boundaries of our State so fair,
Hurrah! hurrah!
Surprise all people everywhere,
Such riches vast containing.
Hurrah! hurrah! the grand young State of Texas!
Hurrah! hurrah! the grand young State of Texas!

And the growth of great men will Texas nourish,
For she is aroused to make her schools flourish.
Then hurrah! hurrah! hurrah! sing we all.

We will make our schools unto none the second,
The best let them soon through the world be reckoned.
Then hurrah! hurrah! hurrah! sing we all.

Cultured minds and hearts be the lovely graces
For crowning the beauty of fair Texas faces.
Then hurrah! hurrah! hurrah! sing we all.

Come and join our song in a glad rejoicing,
With glorious zeal together all voicing.
Then hurrah! hurrah! hurrah! sing we all.

Fig. 30

The organization of the Music Teachers National Association in 1876 and that of the Music section of the National Education Association in 1884 were quickly reflected in Texas by the organization at Austin in 1886 of the Texas Music Teachers' Association, with 76 members. Its object was to unite the musical profession "for better protection of its interests, fraternal feeling, improvement in methods of teaching and a higher degree of musical culture throughout the state," and to work in cooperation with the national body. The moving spirit of the organization was J. Alleine Brown of Chappell Hill, who was vice-president for Texas of the national association; its secretary during the ten years of the existence of the organization was William Besserer of Austin. After some five years of

(83)

continued growth, the membership declined and the attendance at the annual meetings became so limited that it was permitted to expire after 1894. Its membership was made up almost exclusively of private teachers of music, largely piano, although some of the private schools were represented. Its rolls give no indication of any alliance of its interests with the teachers of music in the public schools, who were still few in number.

Before 1900 such instruction in music as was given at public expense was, as was true of the United States in general, limited to vocal music; but in contrast with the programs of the larger cities, Texas adopted no uniform course of study, such as Luther Mason's *National Course,* whose popularity was extensive. Few were the attempts at systematic teaching of even the fundamentals of music except in the schools which employed special music teachers, and these were usually visiting members of the staff, not a part of the regular faculty. Only in the German schools was music taught systematically through the grades. In the public high schools, which came into existence after 1880, no music was taught for many years.

Very slowly, with the opening of the 20th century, was the system inaugurated in the larger cities of having a music supervisor teach the regular class-room teachers, who, in turn, attempted to teach the children. Certain defects became at once apparent; there were few musicians trained for public school work; and many class-room teachers, good in other subjects lacked both voice and ear for music. To obviate the latter difficulty, any teacher in a school found especially fitted either by nature or training to conduct the music classes, was permitted to exchange with the other teachers who could not. In the Anglo-American schools the movable-do system was uniformly followed and the textbooks used were of American origin; in the foreign schools, where the best work was done, the fixed-do system prevailed and foreign textbooks were the rule. Vocal music was the only type known to the schools.

While progress, if somewhat slow and halting, was thus being made in Texas, Thomas Edison was at work on his sound-reproducing machine, for which he secured his first patent in 1877. So slow was its improvement, that even after fifteen years the reproduced tone was so faint as to be inaudible to all but the person connected with the machine by a transmitter to his ear. In the nineties these machines reached Texas, where they were regarded with great curiosity. Phonograph parlors were instituted as a form of amusement. Each machine was provided with from six to eight pairs of transmitters; the auditor held them to his ear in an attempt to catch sounds which appeared to come as from a great distance, accompanied with much creaking and groaning of the apparatus. Musicians scoffed at such music; and educators could not, at the time, foresee any application to their field of this still crude toy.

Piece by piece the sound reproducing machine was perfected. The early wax cylinder gave way to circular discs; friction was gradually eliminated; the tone quality was improved; and the recording done by electrical methods. Before all these improvements had been worked out, educators had begun to sense the increasing importance for them of the machine. In 1896 Springfield, Massachusetts, introduced an appreciation course in music, made possible through the illustrations furnished by the machines; and by 1910 such instruction was being given in Texas, if not in as organized a form. Year by year thereafter the phonograph advanced from the kindergarten to the college, until it became a daily disseminator of, and a contributor to, the understanding of music as an art.

The Vacant Chair.

From *The Silver Lute.*

FIG. 31

BOOK III

THE PERIOD OF
AMALGAMATION

CHAPTER XI

Effects of the World War on Musical Progress

THE years preceding the entry of the United States into the World War served for Texas as a period of initiation, for conditions in Mexico necessitated the transit of large bodies of troops from all parts of the country to and through Texas. The occupation of Vera Cruz in 1915 seemed an echo of the events of 1846-1848; the Pershing expedition into Mexico and the contacts of the Federal troops stationed along the Rio Grande, where bandits and revolutionists kept all astir for years, brought into Texas a flood of Mexican airs and revolutionary songs. Some of these came in printed form; many more, through oral transmission.

The entrance of the United States into the European mêlée ushered in an era of community singing never before known in Texas. The songs most commonly used were the patriotic and those already generally familiar; the new war songs sung in Texas during that particular period are the subject of a special study not yet complete.* Certain ones, such as "Smiles," "Pack up your troubles," and "There's a Long, Long Trail a-winding," attained great popularity in all the army camps; of these Camp Travis at San Antonio was easily the greatest in the Southwest. The encouragement of community singing in the camps had both good and bad results. Men who had never sung before and who had looked upon music as something quite beneath their dignity, now, under the influence of the crowd, joined wholeheartedly. So far, so good. But both this singing, which became quite a popular pastime, and the music played by the military bands were turned directly to the one end desired by political and military leaders—that of arousing a public sentiment which would support the war program. In accomplishing this, the music program sponsored

---

*Dr. Milton Gutsch of the History Department of the University of Texas, with rare foresight, gathered a remarkably complete collection of documents showing the relation of Texas to the World War. These will furnish many detailed studies for future historians.

by the War Department emphasized Americanization so drastically that the enthusiasm of the foreign elements for their own music was, unfortunately, completely destroyed.

Not only music suffered as a result of the Americanization program; foreign languages were swept from the curriculum of the graded school. At the very time that a child is most susceptible to a cultivation of the sense for language, such instruction was prohibited. German, which had, for a half century, been taught in the public schools of San Antonio from the third grade on, and Spanish, usually taught from the fifth, were eliminated by legislative enactment. French, taught only in a few high schools, was but slightly affected; in the secondary schools the enrollment veered toward Spanish. But now, for the first time in Texas, the child of foreign ancestry was made to feel ashamed of it. Even in towns like New Braunfels in which German had been the language of the people since its establishment in 1845, the teachers were so carried away by war propaganda or fear of criticism, that children were made afraid to address their parents at home in the tongue they had formerly used. To such extremes did otherwise intelligent people go that, in an excess of patriotic fervor, they consigned ruthlessly to the flames German libraries and collections of music which were priceless from an historical standpoint, as they covered, in some instances, the whole period of German life in Texas. The drafting of young men who were descendants of foreign immigrants had the further effect of sundering forever the bonds of blood and language which had united them with Europe. The severing of these relations was promptly reflected in the commercial world. Books and music, formerly imported, and sung in foreign tongues, were replaced by others printed in the United States in the English langugage. In only too many cases, the former contacts with sources of the best of foreign music and literature were broken, never to be restored in the same fashion.

The effects of the war propaganda on the young children of Germanic descent were soon perceptible. After being taught in their most impressionable years that their European relatives were monsters capable of committing the most horrible atrocities, many grew up with a horror of all things German; they were ashamed to admit understanding the language, much less using it. Foreign-born parents were replied to in English; foreign books, pictures, even music were regarded with scorn. As the schools conducted in a foreign language were entirely closed for a time, and only slowly, as people recovered from the general hysteria, reopened, thousands of children who had spoken readily a foreign tongue lost their command of it entirely. As a result of this drastic program, the songs their ancestors had sung and cherished were discarded; the ranks of the musical organizations the parents had fostered were never filled by the sons and daughters. A gap was opened between two generations, never to be bridged.

Nowhere were the results more noticeable than in the fields of literature and music in Texas. In the higher institutions of learning, the special classes open to students who commanded a speaking knowledge of a foreign tongue were discontinued, for the students entering could neither speak nor read anything but English. The rich background of folk song and dance had also been lost, and nothing substituted therefor.

Other drastic changes which banished music from the social life of the foreign element in Texas, especially among the laboring classes, were brought about through prohibition, which was made possible largely through the war conditions prevailing at the time of the passage of this measure. It closed the old German beer-hall and the beer-garden, where music and social enjoyment had advanced so comfortably hand in hand through the years. During the period of prohibition, most of these places disappeared, never to be restored. Gone were the resorts where the family went together on Sunday afternoons; gone, too, was the habit of the family staying together.

Especially were these changes reflected in the German singing societies, whose history we shall now briefly retrace.

CHAPTER XII

Singing Societies in Texas

THE earliest singng societies of which we have a record in the early annals of Texas were not composed of Germans; they were made up of Anglo-Americans. The call for the organization of the first of these was issued at Houston late in 1839. The organization was effected, and the society functioned for a time, according to bits culled from the local press of the era. It served more as a choir for the religious services held in the capitol than as a secular choral group, but enlisted in its ranks were people sufficiently interested in music to attempt to promote a better type of sacred music than was generally current. Beginning late in 1850, the Austin Serenaders, a group of male singers, gave a series of concerts at the capital city. A musical association was formed in Dallas in 1856 of which we have a few details; one in Houston, organized in 1857 was broader in design, as it included both sacred and secular vocal and instrumental music on its programs. There existed, no doubt, other Anglo-American

Sacred Music Society.—We have been requested to invite those ladies and gentlemen of this city who are anxious to form a society for the purpose of improving themselves in Sacred music, to assemble on Thursday evening next, at 7 1-2 o'clock, in the Representative Hall.—The importance of such a society will present itself to every individual, who will reflect a moment on the subject. Singing is one of the most interesting parts of public worship and as such has received particular attention in all Christian countries; and in the Northern United States, is now one of the prominent branches of study in many schools. It is indispensable to the agreeable and effective performance of this portion of divine worship, that those who desire to participate in it should have at least a little knowledge of the rules and principles of music; else its soothing effect will be lost, by want of harmony, time, &c. In addition to this, there is another strong reason why such a society should be organized. Most persons, particularly the young, take pleasure in singing, or in listening; and it has now become a well known fact, that individuals need not be born singers, but that the human voice is as susceptible of cultivation and improvement as the human mind. An innocent and agreeable method of passing some of the long winter evenings, is thus presented to those—and we trust there are many such—who prefer amusement of this nature, to those which tend alike to injure the normal and intellectual character. We confidently expect to see a numerous attendance.

FIG 32

groups in the same era, but little is known of their activities.

The German singing society in Texas* was the outgrowth of a movement in Germany which culminated in the formation of the first German National Saengerfest at Frankfort-on-the-Main in July, 1838, when over 700 singers participated. As

FIG 33

The First German Singing Society in Texas, the Germania, organized in New Braunfels, March 2, 1850. This drawng was made by Carl G. Iwonsky, in 1857. The members pictured above are (reading around the table from the left): August Bechstedt, A. Baier, Ed Rische, F. Moreau, H. Conring, C. H. Holtz, Julius Bremer, H. Seele, E. von Stein, G. Eisenlohr, A. Schlameus, J. Rennert, A. Hartmann and H. Schimmelpfennig.

an echo of that program, there was organized at New Braunfels on March 2nd, 1850, the Germania, the first German singing society in the state.

Soon afterward similar groups were formed at Austin, San Antonio and Sisterdale, a tiny hamlet in the hills. On October 15, 1853, these four groups met in the First Saengerfest at New Braunfels. Torrential rains made the trip almost

*To some extent I have followed the "Brief History of the German State Saengerbund of Texas" in Moritz Tiling's *German Element in Texas*(Houston, 1913), but the possession of the original programs collected by Carl Besserer of Austin (1850-1931) has enabled me to make certain corrections and enlargements.

Lebewohl.

FRIEDRICH SILCHER, 1831.

1. Mor - gen muss ich fort von hier und muss Ab - schied neh - men.
2. Wenn zwei gu - te Freun - de sind, die ein - an - der ken - nen,
3. Küs - set dir ein Lüf - te - lein Wan - gen o - der Hän - de,

O du al - ler - schön - ste Zier, Schei - den, das bringt Grä - men.
Sonn' und Mond be - we - gen sich, e - he sie sich tren - nen.
den - ke, dass es Seuf - zer sein, die ich zu dir sen - de.

Da ich dich so treu ge - liebt, ü - ber al - le Ma - ssen,
Noch viel grö - sser ist der Schmerz, wenn ein treu - ver - lieb - tes Herz
Tau - send schick' ich täg - lich aus, die da we - hen um dein Haus,

soll ich dich ver - las - sen, soll ich dich ver - las - sen!
in die Frem - de zie - het, in die Frem - de zie - het.
weil ich dein ge - den - ke, weil ich dein ge - den - ke.

FIG 34

The selection sung at the first Texas Saengerfest (1853) by the Austin group.

impossible; the Austin singers lost their books and supplies while swimming the swollen Blanco River; the Saenger-
halle could be reached from the town only by wagon; yet
everybody was there. The director of the San Antonio group
was Adolf Douai, editor of the San Antonio *Staatszeitung*
and prominent later outside the state as a writer; A. Siemering
directed the Sisterdale group; H. Guenther of New Braunfels,
the Germania; while the Austinites were led by G. Petmecky.
The program, which well deserves to figure in the annals of
music in Texas was as follows:

PART I

Vaterlandslied A Marschner Mass chorus
Liebeschmerz Volkscng Austin Society
Minnelied, J. Otto Germania Singing Society
Der Tanz, J. Otto San Antonio Society
Das treue deutsche herz by J. Otto Germania
Trinklied C. Kreutzer Sisterdale Quartette

PART II

An die Freundschaft, A Neithardt Mass chorus
Lebewohl F. Silcher Austin Society
Auf dem Wasser zu singen by Goethe Sisterdale Quartette
Schlosserlied, by J. Otto, Germania Singing Society
Was ist des Deutschen Vaterland, by Cotta, San Antonio
Singing Society
Jaegers Abschied Mendelssohn Mass Chorus

The second Saengerfest was held the next year at San Antonio with the same organizations participating. We are not
concerned here with the political activities of these groups;
but the fact that the meetings gave opportunity for organized
expression on many public questions should not be overlooked.
At San Antonio a constitution of the Saengerbund was offered
for adoption, and the leaders seized the occasion to express
themselves upon various public questions, notably on slavery
and public education.

By 1855 there were thirteen German singing societies in
the state, but only Indianola, Columbus and La Grange, in addition to those already named, took part in the third meeting
at New Braunfels. After Austin declined the honor of acting
as host for the next year, the Austin, San Antonio and La
Grange groups met again at New Braunfels as guests of a
newly organized society, the *Liedertafel*. Here for the first
time the songs were accompanied, a piano taking the place of
the original orchestral accompaniment to "Eine Nacht auf dem

Meere," a choral work which included solos and duets. The fifth meeting was also held at New Braunfels with only four societies attending, as the Sisterdale group had dissolved; the sixth was at Fredericksburg, then a frontier outpost, with two groups from New Braunfels and one each from Austin, San Antonio, Fredericksburg, Pedernales and Grape Creek taking part. At the seventh Saengerfest, held at New Braunfels in March, 1860, a mixed chorus participated for the first time— this was the *Concordia* of New Braunfels. The meeting planned for Austin for 1861 was, due to war conditions, not held.

Not until 1869 was an attempt made to revive the Saengerfest; in that year representatives from the two San Antonio groups, the Beethoven Maennerchor and the Liedertafel, the Austin Germania, and a group from Boerne prepared a new constitution and selected San Antonio as the next place of meeting. In September, 1870, the eighth Saengerfest was held there in a jubilant spirit, for the Franco-Prussian War had brought victory to the Germans. Although there were German singing societies in both Houston and Galveston, only groups from west of the Colorado participated: the two New Braunfels groups, Boerne, Comfort, Yorktown, La Grange, and San Antonio. It was then decided to hold the meetings only biennially. At the 1872 meeting the establishment of singing schools for children was recommended, and for many years such schools were conducted in various cities and towns of South Texas. Not only children of German parentage but also those of other ancestry were instructed; and from their ranks came, in many cases, the later members of the singing societies.

The eleventh Saengerfest at San Antonio in 1877 marked the initial appearance of soloists and an orchestra in connection with the massed chorus. *Meeresstille* by Fischer and parts of Rossini's *Stabat Mater* were given. From this meeting dated the attempt of each city to outdo its predecessor in the matter of orchestra and soloists; singers from New York and orchestras from Cincinnati, St. Louis, Chicago and Minneapolis were imported to add splendor to the programs.

At the twelfth Saengerfest, held in Austin in 1879, the

twenty-fifth anniversary of the founding of the State Saengerbund was celebrated.

PROGRAM OF 12TH SAENGERFEST, AUSTIN, 1879

PART I

Overture Egmont by Beethoven, Orchestra
Lob des Gesanges by L. Maurer, Mass Chorus
Zauber der Liebe, J. Herbert, Salamander, Galveston
Das Deutsche Lied by P. E. Schneider, Mass Chorus
    and Orchestra
Das Einsame Roeslein, by Hermes, Germania, Brenham
Phantassie, Die Zigeunerin, by Balfe, Orchestra

PART II

Siegesfeuer by Rheinlander, Mass Chorus
Chor aus Ernani by Verdi, Mixed Chorus, Austin
Potpouri, Aïda by Verdi, Orchestra
Wie hab ich sie geliebt by Moehring, Frohsinn, Dallas
Schaeferlied by Eckert, Mass Chorus

PART III

Leichte Cavallerie by Suppé, Orchestra
Muttersprache by C. Kuntze, Beethoven, San Antonio
Bundeslied by F. Lachner, Mass Chorus and Orchestra
Song by New Braunfels Maennerchor
Fackeltanz No. 3 by Meyerbeer, Orchestra

Here were present for the last time the organizations from
New Braunfels, Comfort and other towns further west, as
they had formed the "Mountain Singing Union," which has
persisted to the present day. The Austin program was also
marked by the presence for the first time of organizations from
Dallas and Brenham, and the promise of participation by the
Houston Maennerchor.

From this time on the meetings revolved between Dallas,
Galveston, Houston, and San Antonio. The first at Dallas
was in 1883. At the twentieth held at Houston in 1894, three
Anglo-American groups participated for the first time. These
were the "Musical Union" of Austin, directed by Carl Besserer,
also director of the Austin *Saengerrunde;* the "Quartette
Society" of Houston, and the "Quartette Society" of Galveston. Only Texas musicians played in the orchestra or
took part as soloists.

The presence of the Anglo-American groups is an evidence
of the gradual fusion of interests which had been going on
in the larger cities. In Houston an organization known as the

(97)

Philharmonic Society was established as early as 1872 by Mrs. Lucy Grünewald; this was composed of from thirty to forty mixed voices. Mr. Grünewald had a music store in Houston; their granddaughter Lucy Hickenlooper, later known as Olga Samaroff, is a pianist of note and the wife of Stokowski of the Philadelphia Symphony. In 1885 the Houston Choral Club was organized for the purpose of giving musical plays and light operas. In 1894 the gentlemen of that city organized a male quartet club which functioned until 1915; Anton Diehl was the first director and H. T. Huffmaster the last. The first woman's singing society was the Treble Clef, 1895-1900, which was followed by the Woman's Choral Club, active for many years.

THE WOMAN'S CHORAL CLUB, HOUSTON

FIG 35

Even before the formation in 1877 of the second German singing society in Austin, Mrs. Fanny L. Crooker, director of the choir of St. David's Episcopal Church, had organized a singing group which she directed until her death in 1886. In 1888 the "Musical Union" was formed; this lasted over a decade, but directed its efforts largely to the production of opera. Noteworthy was the presentation of Mendelssohn's *Lorelei*, first given in Vienna in 1881, and in this Texas town only a few years later. The Turn Verein also maintained a singing society of which L. Klappenbach was director for many years.

At Dallas the Musical Society, organized as early as 1876,

included the most acocomplished vocalists; it was functioning
in 1883 as the Ladies Musical Society. Galveston had a Philharmonic Society in 1874; and the Mozartina and Island City
Glee Clubs, under the direction of Profesor H. Leberman, also
included singers of other nationalities than German.

After the turn of the century the Saengerfests continued
uninterruptedly until 1916, that at Houston in 1913 being
especially noteworthy in that the selections for the mass
choruses were entirely by American composers, two of whom,
Hans Harthan of Austin and Frank Renard of Sherman, were
citizens of Texas. Twenty-one singing societies were present,
the whole being directed by Arthur Claasen, who was shortly
afterward engaged as director of the Beethoven Maennerchor
of San Antonio and the 1916 Saengerfest. For this occasion
soloists were imported, but the orchestra, largely of local talent, had been organized well in advance. Joined with the
men's voices was the Mozart Society, a San Antonio group of
women's voices of superior quality. With great brilliance the
thirtieth Saengerfest was celebrated. That occasion marked
the greatest height to which the German singing societies in
Texas attained, either in point of number of societies, voices,
or excellence of performance.

Another year and the United States was at war with Germany. The German singing societies, composed largely of
men, were necessarily disbanded. The effect of public sentiment during the war on German music has already been point-
ed out. The anti-German feeling which persisted after the
treaty of Versailles prevented reorganization for a time; in San
Antonio a group was brought together in 1921 in order to give a
concert for German relief. The next year a small group assembled at Austin in an attempt to resuscitate the old German-
American spirit; the results were disheartening. Not until 1929
was a Saengerfest held; this meeting in San Antonio was attended by the survivors of the Beethoven Maennerchor, the
Liederkranz, and a mixed chorus of the Sons of Hermann from
San Antonio; groups from New Braunfels, Austin, Taylor,
Houston, Galveston, Schulenberg, and Uhland;—some 300
voices— under the direction of H. Jacobson of Rochester, New
York. In 1932 the Mountain Singers, then a fifty-one-year-old

representative of the Germans from New Braunfels westward, gave a concert in San Antonio.

In all of these meetings the fact that young blood was lacking was all too apparent. Either because they knew no German, had lost contact with the past of their ancestors, or because the new age had left no place for such a form of recreation, the young man no longer slipped in beside the father. Although the older men have held on, some of the organizations have already ceased to exist. Clearly the death knell of the German singing society has been sounded, and it can be only a few years before that institution will have become only a tradition in the musical annals of Texas; for in a short time few records will remain of one of the strongest factors in the cultural development of the state.

A survey of the activities of these various groups brings out a few facts of special interest. One of these is the very slow growth of organizations of women's voices. After 1880 a mixed chorus was usually organized in the city which was to entertain the next Saengerfest; this included all singers willing to take part. But separate organizations of women's voices intended to be permanent were rare among the Germans. The Mozart Society, organized by Arthur Claasen as a sister group to the Beethoven Maennerchor, is one of the few survivors. The use of school children for choral purposes dates from 1891, when the children of Comfort sang four-part songs at a meeting of the Mountain Singers. At Houston in 1913 and at San Antonio in 1916 and 1929 large groups of public school children joined in the choruses. In the last meetings, members of the high school orchestras have taken places in the chairs of the Saengerfest orchestra.

In these children, whose sole instruction is that given in the public schools of Texas, lies hope for the continuance of choral singing in the future. The old traditions, the old spirit of comradeship within the small group of kindred spirits linked by ties of blood and language, have gone. In their place something new must be created; perhaps it is already in the making. But at the point in the road at which the new branches off from the old, a backward glance offers the conviction that during almost a century the German singing society served a most worthy purpose and deserves no small place in the history of musical culture in Texas.

CHAPTER XIII

The Opera in Texas

REMOTE as Texas was from the musical centers of North America before the building of railroads, it is surprising with what speed operas traveled in whole or in excerpts to her borders. One of the most popular ballads from *Fra Diavolo,* first produced at Paris in 1830, was sung on the Texas stage in 1838 and passed at once into the permanent repertoire of the singers of the state (See Figure 36).

Through the next two decades bits of opera of various types crept into Texas in some form. The March from *Norma* was popularized though the music of the Mexican War. Among the operatic excerpts which reached Texas before the Civil War, were songs from Fry's *Leonora;* Bellini's *Sonnambula;* the *Postillion of Lonjumeau; Cinderella;* Bishup's *Guy Mannering;* and Balfe's *Daughter of St. Mark* and *The Enchantress,* in addition to the well known *Bohemian Girl* and Wallace's *Maritana.** In addition to the solo selections, duets, trios, and choruses from these and similar operas were known in Texas almost as soon as in New Orleans, where the French opera reigned supreme.

The first company organized expressly for opera which played on Texas soil was the German opera company which came to Galveston from St. Louis in 1856 and gave at Lone Star Hall acts from several operas to make up a performance. The first opera given in Texas was in German. During the same decade Galveston was visited by the French opera, and in 1857 there was an Italian opera company from Mexico at Brownsville, which is not surprising as the Mexicans had, from their first contact with Italian Opera in 1833, shown themselves enthusiastic devotees of that type. These auspicious beginnings of opera in Texas were rudely cut short by the Civil War.

Late in the sixties operas were again being given, both by local talent and visiting companies. In 1869 the Marie Frederici company gave *Martha, Fra Diavolo,* and the *Magic Flute*

---

*Copies of these, brought to Texas largely before 1853, are in the possession of the writer.

ON YONDER ROCK RECLINING

ZERLINA.

On yon-der rock re-clin-ing, That fierce and swar-thy form be-hold; Fast his hands his

car-bine hold, 'Tis his best friend of old! This way his steps in-clin-ing, His

scar-let plume waves o'er his brow, And his vel-vet cloak hangs low, Playing in grace-ful

flow! Trem . . . . . . ble! E'en while the storm is beat-ing, A-far hear Echo re-

peat-ing, Diavolo! Diavolo! Diavolo! Trem . . . . . . ble!

E'en while the storm is beat - - - ing, A - far hear E - cho re - peat - - ing,

Dia-vo-lo! Dia-vo-lo! Dia-vo-lo! Diavolo!

Diavolo! Diavolo!

Although his foes waylaying
He fights with rage and hate combin'd,
Towards the gentle fair they find
He's ever mild and kind:
The maid too heedless straying
(For one we Pietro's daughter know)
Home returns full sad and slow,
What can have made her so?
Tremble! each one the maiden meeting
Is sure to be repeating,
Diavolo! Diavolo! Diavolo!

Diavolo. While thus his deeds accusing,
Let justice too at least be shown;
All that's lost here, let us own,
Mayn't be his prize alone:
Full of his name abusing,
Perchance some young and rustic beau,
Whilst with love he feigns to glow
At beauty's shrine bows low!
Tremble! each sighing lover dread,
For of him more truly may be said,
Diavolo! Diavolo! Diavolo!

FIG 36

First operatic selection sung on the concert stage in Texas

at Houston, and that same year Partido's Mexican troupe visited San Antonio, Austin, New Braunfels, Seguin, Brenham, Houston and Galveston. Selections from opera were frequently offered on concert programs. At Austin, at a benefit concert, the Overtures to *Fra Diavolo* and *Wiliam Tell* were given, and among the songs were "Tyrant Burst thy Chains" from the *Barber of Seville;* an air and chorus from *Masaniello;* "Sweet Spirit Hear My Prayer" from Wallace's *Lurline;* "Through yon Window" from *Lucrecia Borgia;* "Ernani, Rescue Me" from *Ernani;* and "Ill Sustaining the Encounter" from *Il Trovatore.* Shortly afterward the first scene from *Don Giovanni* and the first act of *Der Freischutz* were given with a large orchestra and chorus under the direction of Julius Schutze.

Before 1870 the state boasted only theaters and music halls, but with the erection of the Tremont Opera House in Galveston in 1871 the era of the opera house as the home of the best in drama and music begins. In the eighties Dallas, Austin and San Antonio each had an opera house; all of these have gone; even a later one in Austin is today a moving-picture house. At the Tremont in Galveston in 1872 an operatic concert was given at which selections from *Il Trovatore, Lucia, Il Puritani,* and *Ernani* were given with orchestral accompaniment under the direction of Mr. Maddern. The first production in this class by local talent was in 1876 when "The Feast of Roses," an operetta in three scenes, the text by Mollie Moore Davis, later famed as a poet, and music by William Kepler, was presented and favorably received. Dallas' first opera with an orchestra was *Martha,* directed by Professor Otten at Field's Theater on February 12,1875; *Il Trovatore* followed shortly with the leading rôles filled by Miss Ella Rives, Dr. J. W. McGee, Mrs. Ben Ward, Major Obenchain, and Mr. Hess, while the best amateur talent of the city figured in the choruses and orchestra. Saulsbury's "Troubadours" gave the comic opera *Patchwork* there in 1876, and continued to return to Texas every year until late in the nineties. The banner year of musical life in Dallas before 1900 was 1883, in which the new opera house, with a parterre and galleries seating 1200, was opened with a performance of *Iolanthe,* a Gilbert and Sullivan success. Here opera, with the best of the drama, flourished until the building was destroyed by fire in

1901. A new one at once took its place.

The extent to which the "Little Opera," if we may so parallel the popular use of the term "Little Theater," flourished in Texas, even before the coming of the railroads, is generally little realized. Yet in a town as small as Austin, opera by local talent was no rare event. From the return of William Besserer, born there in 1850 but sent to Germany to study during the Civil War, dates a period in which some group of singers was constantly busy rehearsing or giving opera. Many of the scores used are now in the possession of the writer: among these are *Olivette, Nanon, Chimes of Normandy, Maid Marion, Robin Hood, Czar und Zimmerman, Princess Ida, The Pretty Chanticleer, Sonnambula, Love's Vow, Nachtlager in Granada, Stradella, Martha, Mikado, Pinafore, Il Trovatore,* and *Faust.* The orchestra was drawn from local musicians, occasionally assisted by a few from Houston or San Antonio. In the main, though, Austin is typical of the small Texas town with a substantial German population: it created its own amusements, and one of the favored forms was opera.

Another group of organizations that sponsored light opera with local talent was made up of the Turner Societies. This practice was followed in both large and small communities. the Turners thus contributing to the general culture of the group. One of their functions was the promotion of song among the younger members, and these performances furnished a definite end toward which to work. In San Antonio, the Turner group contributed not only the performances but the main theater, for Turner Hall, which occupied the site of the present Brady Building, was for more than thirty years the center of drama and music in that city. The Casino had a small stage on which operas and operettas were presented, largely by the German element.

The extension of railroads to San Antonio early in the eighties made it possible for opera companies of national fame to reach both that city and Austin. During the season of 1887-88 we find the Carleton Opera Company and that of Emma Abbott booked; the following year the Faust Opera Company and Campanini's troupe gave performances in both cities after a series in Dallas. It was these towns, with Houston and Galveston—the ones that entertained the Saengerfest—that were usually visited by touring companies.

The practice of having a few visiting opera companies each year give one or more performances continues to the present day, but the practice of depending on local talent has become more and more general among the non-German population. Bits from the musical annals between 1915 and 1919 will illustrate something of this trend, although war years can scarcely be regarded as typical. In May, 1915, *Martha* was given at Plainview; *Pinafore* at Amarillo in January, 1916. In March, came the Boston opera with *Pagliacci, Butterfly,* and *L'Amore de tre re* to Dallas. In April, Carl Venth's *Fair Betty*—a comic opera— was given by local talent in Fort Worth. In Houston, Van Hoose formed an operatic society to give *Cavalleria*. Marshall presented the *Egyptian Princess;* Amarillo repeated *Pinafore*. In October the Ellis grand opera company gave *Carmen* and *Il Trovatore* at Fort Worth; in the following January the Boston Company, *Faust, Iris, Aïda* at Dallas, and *Aïda* and *La Bohême* at Austin. In 1917 *Faust* was given at Fort Worth by local talent, while a community opera company at Waxahachie gave *Priscilla,* and *Faust* and *Lucia* were given at Houston. Creatore's company gave *Cavalleria* and *Pagliacci* at Waco early in 1919; in June the *Mikado* was reported from Cleburne; the Scotti company gave *Cavalleria* and *L'Oraculo* at Dallas; and the Chicago, *Aïda, Butterfly,* and *La Bohême* at Fort Worth. In that same year Rafaelo Diaz, the son of a San Antonio cigar manufacturer, was engaged to sing at the Metropolitan, and shortly afterward Josephine Lucchesi of the same city was starred by the San Carlo Company.

Since 1920 the disconnected efforts to support opera have fused to some extent, especially in San Antonio, Dallas, and Houston, in an effort to develop municipal opera. In general, the traveling opera company as a feature of musical life is fast disappearing. All indications point to the future development of opera through sound pictures and the establishment of municipally-financed productions through the use of local talent for at least the minor rôles and the chorus. There is no question that the raw material is at hand; it only requires training and wise direction. As more capable teachers and directors control the field, there seems small doubt that the opera of the future in Texas will be sung either by international stars in sound pictures or by Texas singers.

CHAPTER XIV

The Symphony Orchestra in Texas

THE first steps toward the development of the symphony orchestra in Texas are to be sought in the records of the German singing societies, for it was the need of an orchestra as the background for a successful Saengerfest that led to the formation of larger instrumental groups in various parts of the state. While the first programs of these singers were entirely unaccompanied, such conditions did not endure long; even by 1855 the piano was substituting for the orchestra. But not until 1877 did a group of instrumentalists appear; in that year Mr. Zawadil gathered thirty-four players at San Antonio for the performance of orchestral music at the Saengerfest; they gave the overtures from *The Bohemian Girl, Martha,* and *Nebuchadnezzar* by Verdi, and played the accompaniment for Fischer's *Meeresstille* and Rossini's *Stabat Mater.* From this date, the orchestra, either local or imported, was regarded as an indispensable adjunct. In 1879 Austin brought an orchestra from New Orleans, which assisted in a program under the direction of Walter Tips. This practice of engaging soloists and orchestra from larger cities did not meet the approval of the director of the twentieth Saengerfest at Houston; he selected only Texas musicians to play in the orchestra or sing the solos. His example was not followed; when the twenty-ninth Saengerfest was held at Houston in 1913 the St. Louis Symphony orchestra with fifty-five men under Max Zach was imported.

This demand for an orchestral group united local musicians who afterwards held together as a body for longer or shorter periods. Groups from the different towns were sometimes united with a few specially imported players for some of the Saengerfests. By the late eighties the larger towns that entertained the Saengerfest had developed groups of from eighteen to thirty men, who played together with some degree of regularity. In Austin, Herzog, who was later succeeded by Besserer; in Galveston, Zawadil for a time; in Dallas,

Kreissig; and in San Antonio, Zawadil, William Marx and Carl Beck directed groups that played music of good composers. The 1885 Saengerfest program at Houston included the *Tannhaüser* Overture of Wagner; and other music of symphonic proportions found its way to the Texas public.

Still it was not until after the turn of the century that Texas turned seriously to the business of developing and supporting a symphony orchestra. In San Antonio, the instigator seems to have been Mrs. Eli Hertzberg, who saw in Carl Hahn, an able musician, one suited to such a purpose. Under his direction the San Antonio Symphony Orchestra was organized in 1904 and continued for some years with a certain degree of success. In 1914 Hahn succeeded to the post of director of the Arion Singing Society of Brooklyn, vacated by Arthur Claasen who accepted the directorship of the Beethoven Maennerchor at San Antonio. At once the newcomer took up the fallen reins. Aided by Mrs. Hertzberg and a committee of San Antonio women, Claasen gathered around him the best players of orchestral instruments, both men and women; he augmented his forces for the concert season with imported professionals for oboe, bassoon, tuba, double bass and tympani. In 1914-15 he gave eight concerts, and the next season also proved a success musically if not financially. At its close the ladies composing the board of directors selected another director for the orchestra Claasen had so painstakingly organized and trained; he himself organized the Philharmonic Symphony Society, and continued for a time to furnish San Antonio with symphonic music of a high type. An able director and competent musician, he nevertheless lacked the business ability demanded of a manager of such a project. At the end of the season he was forced to abandon the field, leaving it to Julian Blitz, who conducted the San Antonio Symphony from 1916 until 1922. After paying a defiicit of some $18,000, the managing board then found it impossible to secure adequate advance support. Since that time there have been resuscitations of the organization, but none permanently effectual.

The Symphony Orchestra in Texas

The Dallas Symphony* can be traced indirectly back to Hans Kreissig, who came to that city in the late eighties, and directed string ensembles around the opening of the century; but directly to Walter Fried who in 1911 founded the Beethoven Symphony Orchestra, which boasted forty players. Carl Venth was secured as director, a post he filled until 1914, but,

FIG 37

THE DALLAS SYMPHONY ORCHESTRA IN ITS EARLY YEARS

as in San Antonio, the undertaking proved expensive for its promoters. In 1918 Mr. Fried again organized a group, the Dallas Symphony, which gave concerts, using the local musicians as soloists. This organization continued until 1924, when he declared a sabbatical year, in order to mature future plans. Instead, he died suddenly in 1925.

His associates, however, decided, to carry on. Through the persistence of Arthur Kramer, the organization was continued under the directorship of Van Katwijk, the first concert being given in December, 1925. Until the present day, the orchestra has been maintained on a profesional basis. Among its offerings have been Respighi's "The Pines of Rome," Kalinnikov's

*The facts here briefly summarized are treated more extensively in Robert Marquis', "The Development of the Symphony Orchestra in Texas" (Austin, 1934), unpublished.

G Minor Symphony, the Second Symphony of Howard Hanson, Honegger's "Pacific 231," Polish dances of Tansman, Ravel's Bolero, "Mother Goose" suite, and "La Valse"; Douglas Moore's "Pageant of P. T. Barnum," a movement from a Mahler symphony, and a variety of pieces by Albeniz, De Falla, Debussy and Sibelius. P. G. Van Rooy's "Piet Hein," a Dutch rhapsody, was given its first performance in America in 1927 and was repeated in 1931. Wagner and Tchaikovski music has been given in the profusion demanded by audiences of today.

The Houston orchestra dates from 1913 when Julian Paul Blitz, a Dutch cellist of ability, took charge. He conducted there until called to San Antonio to take over the organization Claasen had built up. In 1916, Paul Bergé succeeded, but after some years the orchestra was disbanded. In 1931 Allesandro effected an organization; the following year Nespoli was imported from Italy by Mrs. John Wesley Graham as director of the Houston opera and orchestra; besides, E. Van Hoose was directing another group known as the Little Symphony. When the present director, Frank St. Leger of the Chicago Opera, took charge in 1933, the Nespoli organization was shattered, while the Little Symphony assumed a less pretentious role. The Houston Symphony Orchestra, as now organized, is composed of about seventy-five men; its program calls for twelve concerts each season. It is supported by patrons who pay $100 a year, sustaining members at $25 and members at $10.

The Fort Worth Symphony was founded by Carl Venth in 1915 with forty-five local professionals, but was disbanded with the advent of the World War when the director became a bandmaster. In 1924 Brooks Morris reorganized the group of about sixty players on a half-professional and half-student basis. During 1933-34 it had approximately seventy-five members. Its matinees for school children were especially noteworthy, but its general usefulness was restricted by the lack of a suitable hall for performances.

As early as 1892 an orchestral organization was attempted at El Paso, under the sponsorship of the McGinty Club; but this group of volunteer players, which never reached symphonic proportions, disbanded in 1905. In 1915 P. J. Gustat began the work of reorganization; in 1920 Anton Navratil conducted; then the orchestra was again disbanded. At various intervals under G. M. Buchanan and Ross V. Steele as conductors, the group was somewhat brought together. H. Arthur Brown of the Juillard Foundation effected a reorganization in 1930; this orchestra with sixty people, mostly amateurs, gives four concerts a season. A junior symphony orchestra directed by William Black is being prepared to take the place of the present players within a few years.

While there are traces of an orchestral group in Amarillo as early as 1904, the present symphony orchestra is the outgrowth of the Philharmonic Music Club, which invited E. B. Hall to become its director in 1927. In 1932 it emerged as the American Philharmonic Orchestra Association. Utilizing the Municipal Auditorium, its fifty-five players, largely amateurs, give six programs a season, at which guest artists are usually presented.

Besides the orchestras of the large cities there have been orchestras denominated "symphony" in various Texas towns for varying periods. Beaumont had such a group in 1919 under the direction of H. F. Chojnachi; Corsicana in January,1917, was supporting such an organization; one was started in Austin in 1917 under the directorship of Frank L. Reed, head of the music department in the University; Waco was under Severin Frank; but all seem to have expired from one cause or another.

From these meager notes it might seem that Texas is hopelessly backward in developing and supporting orchestras of symphonic proportions, but when contrasted with other older states her efforts are not to be despised. There are only four really great orchestras in the whole United States, the New York Philharmonic, the Philadelphia, Boston, and Chicago. Twelve other cities maintain organizations of lesser rank—Atlanta, Buffalo, Cleveland, Detroit, Cincinnati, Denver, Kansas City, Los Angeles, New Haven, St. Louis, San Francisco, and Seattle; but these are all fairly young, and most of them have lived through periods of vicissitudes such as the Texas orchestras have experienced. None are entirely supported through public funds.

During the period of evolution of local groups, many of

these older orchestras have visited Texas and furnished inspiration and incentive. In 1916 the New York Philharmonic made a tour of the state; in 1917 the St. Louis; and in 1918 the Minneapolis Symphony Orchestra paid a visit. In 1920 the Chicago Symphony visited Dallas and the Cincinnati, Houston; in 1921 the New York Philharmonic returned; and in 1922 Rudolph Gans was in Dallas with the body from St. Louis. This routine has largely been maintained since, one or more of the older organizations visiting at least some part of the state each year.

The future of the symphony orchestra in Texas lies largely in the high schools which, with their band masters and orchestral directors are introducing the children in their plastic years to the instruments whose mastery is essential to the maintenance of such an organization. While it may be years before the state can give really artistic performances with local talent, the way has been opened; and in the future the cost of maintaining symphonic orchestras in Texas will be brought within the reach of the average city through the employment of trained local musicians.

CHAPTER XV

Music Education, 1914-1936

WHILE music continued to hold an important place in the curriculum of the private institutions of higher learning in the state, in the University of Texas, established in 1883, music had no place. Only through persistent effort on the part of a few individuals, notably Dr. W. J. Battle, a member of the faculty, was music, for the first time, made a part of the curriculum in 1914. Three courses, one each in harmony, history of music, and analysis, were offered. The response was immediate; enrollment increased; the teaching staff was enlarged; new courses in public school music were added;* and a private institution to give technical instruction under university supervision was authorized. In 1922 admission credit was granted for courses in music pursued in high schools. But soon afterward there was a general slump in the enrollment, due perhaps most directly to the personnel of the teaching staff; difficulties both within and without the institution led the authorities to look with disfavor upon departments with "temperamental" faculties; finally, in 1925, when the university budget had to be trimmed to meet legislative appropriations, the school of music, with others that had given rise to administrative problems, was eliminated.

This experience would suggest to those unfamiliar with the situation that Texas was not yet ready for a real school of music. Other evidence proves such was not the case. The College of Industrial Arts, established at Denton in 1906 for women only, had built up in the intervening period one of the largest departments in the South. In 1919 the legislature appropriated $150,000 for a music building. In 1921 the school reported an enrollment of over six hundred students and a faculty of twenty, actually the foremost in the South. Its growth has continued with the exception of the depression years. The school has drawn, in many instances, students who would have

---

*Representative of the University taste in music is the *Community Song Book* issued in 1918.

gone elsewhere, but were attracted by the facilities offered for the study of music. What this school, now known as the Texas State College for Women, has done, the University of Texas might have far outstripped, had the school of music been under competent direction. A movement is on foot, with the opening of the centennial year, to bring about the re-establishment of a school of music of the first class in connection with the leading educational institution of the South.

The private music teachers of the state were meantime awakening to some of the problems that began to threaten their future. As the public schools took over the teaching of music, the status of the private teacher was menaced, for with the introduction of the credit system in the schools, no child wanted to take anything which did not "count." Hence arose the problem of securing credit for music studied outside of the public school with private teachers; the solution depended apparently upon the establishment of some type of standardization among the teachers as yet untouched by the certification laws of the state. Around 1915, San Antonio, Dallas, and Austin teachers formed local organizations; and in that same year a new state organization was formed at Dallas; this is still functioning more or less actively according to the leadership of its executives. In 1917 when the United States Bureau of Education approved the accrediting by high schools of work done under private teachers, the smaller Texas towns quickly fell into line: Beaumont, El Paso, Port Arthur, and Galveston soon secured recognition from the school authorities for instrumental work done under private teachers; more towns added special teachers and supervisors; and instrumental music, in the form of bands and orchestras, was slowly added to the regular courses offered.

The inclusion of such courses in high schools introduced new problems of accrediting, both by the high school and the higher institutions to which the students proceeded. The accrediting of high school work for college entrance, for many years in the hands of a committee appointed by the University of Texas, was taken over in 1917 by the State Department of Education, to which school administrators naturally turned for assistance in regard to curriculum, accrediting, and standardizing of music. In an effort to solve the many problems relating to music, the State Superintendent, at that time Miss

Annie Webb Blanton, who had no appropriation with which to employ a Music Supervisor, appointed as one of her rural supervisors Miss Elfleda Littlejohn, formerly music supervisor in Galveston, and delegated to her the organization of music in the schools. A course of study was prepared, some standards of accrediting theoretical courses were worked out, and a beginning made at standardizing the institutions in the state which professed to teach music. During fifteen years the State Department, without any special funds for such work, has attempted to carry on a general supervision of the music taught in the schools; but as there has been no single individual in the department, during much of the time, who was either a theoretical or practical musician, the results have been somewhat dubious. Each of the 246 city supervisors of music listed in 1925 was a law unto herself; each reigned supreme in her small realm with none but the local superintendent, who usually knew nothing of music, to say her nay. The courses of study issued by the department were generally the work of some single individual unconnected with the department, and represented the views of an individual rather than the ripened judgment of a group of experienced supervisors.

The first attempt to formulate a music program for the rural and elementary schools of the state is that of L. A. Woods, Superintendent of Public Instruction, who hopes to have every child taught at least ten songs a year; these are to be sung in large choral groups in the larger cities during the Centennial year. The basis of this program, instruction through the use of phonograph records, hardly appeals to the trained music teachers and supervisors of the state, for they realize that while such a program may introduce music into the rural school and the classroom in which the teacher is incompetent to direct singing, it cannot do anything more than lay the most rudimentary foundation for the rural child, who still will not be on a level musically with those who have had even a year of instruction in a good school system. A beginning is being made to bring music within the reach of every child; but no intelligent concerted program of music study for the better schools of the state has been worked out. There is still no real leadership musically emanating from the State Department of Education. This will probably come only after a legislative appropriation for a State Supervisor of Music makes possible the appointment of a thoroughly trained and experienced official.

Another approach to mass instruction in music through the use of sound-reproducing machines, but from the standpoint of appreciation rather than production, was made through the music memory contest. Instituted first in 1906 by C. M. Tremaine as a means of interesting his own children in good music, the idea caught the attention of educators, and soon contests were held in various cities of the United States. The first noted in Texas was in 1919, when one was planned by Mrs. Charles Norton and directed by Miss Alva Lochhead, supervisor of music at Fort Worth. By 1922, 36 towns in Texas conducted such contests as part of the public school work in music. That same year Miss Henrietta Pyle, supervisor at Wichita Falls, introduced the plan to the whole state through the Interscholastic League, a branch of the Extension Division of the University of Texas. In 1923 a State contest was held. From merely memory work, this contest was expanded to include recognition of theme, form, and the tone of the leading orchestral instruments. For this part of the contest unfamiliar records were sent out in sealed packages to the supervisors of the 254 county contests, at their request. To assist the teacher who lacked experience or material, a test service was instituted by which a new set of records is sent each week to the schools subscribing. In this way both teacher and pupil have an abundance of material suitable for training in *music* rather than in memory. In 1932 a choral singing contest, the pioneer of the plan now sponsored by the State Department, was introduced. As a basis for this contest phonograph records served; the songs were very simple, as befitted the rural schools that had previously had no music of any kind. There was an immediate response and the demand has grown.

Although teacher-training courses in music have been offered by all the state-supported teacher-training institutions except the University of Texas, none of of these schools can as yet maintain the standards of a first-class music school. Among the reasons for this are probably the mad rush to increase enrollment regardless of type of student; lack of preparation in music on the part of college students who would like to teach music; and the difficulty of obtaining salary appropriation that would attract the best teachers of the subject. In the public junior college, practically no music courses of value are given; and only a few of the private schools of this type are doing standard work. Three denominational colleges, Southern Methodist University at Dallas, Baylor University at Waco, and Our Lady of the Lake at San Antonio, are the only music schools in the state authorized by the National Association of Music Schools to confer degrees in music. The Incarnate Word College of San Antonio will probably be accepted in 1936; Simmons College is on probation. According to the rating of the State Department of Education, only two private institutions, the Texas School of Fine Arts at Austin and the Fort Worth Conservatory, are recognized as giving courses leading to the special music certificate. Under the laws of Texas, any teacher holding even a second-grade certificate can teach music without ever having had a course in the subject, but the holder of a special music teacher's certificate, although required to have practically two years of general college work, is not authorized to teach anything else.

The private teacher of music is today a relic of an era past; elementary music will be taught in the future in schools to groups, and practical music will become a laboratory course in high schools and colleges. Those able to sense the educational changes that are taking place realize that, during the Centennial year, there are three goals toward which those interested in musical progress in Texas should be striving. The first of these is the establishment of a music school of the first class in connection with the University of Texas; the second, a legislative appropriation and authorization for the employment of a competent State Supervisor of Music; and third, the inclusion, in the requirements for any teacher's certificate,

of at least one course in music.* With these secured, the
road is open for some real progress in musical education in
Texas.

---

*As this goes to press, the news comes that this requirement is to
be made effective in September, 1936, by order of the State Superintendent of Public Instruction, who, although not himself a musician, has
shown a keen realization of the value of music in education. There
is every probability that the Board of Regents of the University of
Texas, supported by the State Federation of Clubs, Music Clubs and
various civic organizations, will include a School of Fine Arts in
its 1937-39 budget requested of the State Legislature.

CHAPTER XVI

Other Agencies Contribuing to Musical Progress

IN awakening an interest in music in the general public, probably no single agency has been more active and effective than the women's clubs of the state. First organized about 1885, these groups interested themselves at first solely in the study of literary subjects; but by 1897, when the State Federation of Women's Clubs was organized, something of their potentiality in other fields was beginning to be realized. Some of these clubs included music on their programs in the early days, but around 1895 groups whose distinct purpose was music study came into existence. As to which is the pioneer, perhaps no one can answer definitely. As a result of the study of a Musical Literary Course prepared by Mr. Derthick of Chicago and introduced into some of the larger towns and cities, a music club was organized in Houston in 1895 by Mr. Sandy Mason, a violinist, Mrs. Edwin B. Baker was president, and Mrs. Ione Allen Peden and Mrs. Baltis Allen were among its members. Navasota formed a similar group in 1899 with Mrs. Laura Blackshear as president and Miss Julia Owen among the members. Until 1915 such music clubs were either separate entities or members of the State Federation of Clubs, which had a Music Department; in 1915 these formed the State Federation of Mucic Clubs, but still retained membership in the General Federation. In 1921 there were seventy-seven clubs so federated, in addition to some who retained membership only in the General Federation.

By 1925 the duplication of fees and other problems led to the complete separation of the two groups. At the opening of 1936 there are over four hundred clubs who are members of the Music Federation and many that are members of the General Federation; some are pursuing courses prepared by the Extension Division of the University of Texas or other educational institutions; and there are a few entirely independent units. The total membership of these various groups, whose common purpose is the study of music and its general advancement in the state, is such that no thinking person can fail to realize the influence they can exert when they wish. Through the programs of the members, sponsorship of guest artists, the encouragement of music in the public schools, the development of community and municipal music, these organizations have exerted an incalculable influence. The large number of concerts sponsored by clubs may be seen from the calendar of the 1920-1921 season in the Appendix. The large constructive leadership these clubs should be of great influence in the future.

Among the professional organizations in the state, the most powerful should be the music section of the State Teachers Association, in existence since 1886, but it has not exerted itself in proportion to its ability. Joined with it should be the membership of the Texas Music Teachers Association, which has functioned since 1915, but whose membership is largely made up of private teachers of limited perspective as regards the whole music program of the state. The Texas Band Masters Association formed in 1922 has been active; credits have been secured for band and orchestral work in the schools, and municipal efforts have been given support. Two other professional groups, the Texas Chapter of the American Guild of Organists, organized at Dallas in 1918 and the Texas Chapter of the American Association of Harpists in 1922 suggest something of progress in both these fields. A Church Music Conference, held annually at Southwestern University at Georgetown since 1928, has had as its purpose the advancement of standards in church music generally.

In the field of civic music Texas has made a beginning. Song leaders and band directors were trained during the World War; at its close some were employed by various agencies. The Dallas Municipal Music Commission appointed in July, 1919, while not the first in the country, was the first established on broad principles and the first to grasp the aims and possibilities of such a body and the true character of democratic musical activities as a public service. This commission has sponsored the Music Memory Contest, Music Day, Music Week, a Municipal Chorus of some two hundred voices accompanied by the Dallas Symphony, sing-songs in the munici-

(120)

pal parks as a feature of band concerts, free Sunday after-
noon concerts, and a spring music festival. At first without
any financial appropriation whatever, the body was later given
$5,000 a year, which under careful apportionment has been
sufficient to keep various musical activities afloat. Other cities
have used this body as a model; Forth Worth early established a Music Commission; Beaumont followed suit in 1922.

Something of the status of music in Texas in 1924 from the
standpoint of municipal encouragement may be gleaned by re-
plies to questionnaires sent out to the mayors of cities of over
5,000 population by the National Bureau for the Advancement
of Music. The figures do not by any means tell all the facts;
like San Antonio, some cities did not reply; others reported no
money spent for music although they actually had well developed school music departments, maintained from school rather
than municipal funds. Most of the mayors who replied were
more than favorable to the encouragement of municipal music,
but stated that lack of funds was the strongest deterrent factor.

In the thirty-two towns* reporting, the municipal appropriation for music ranged from nothing in twenty-one, and $60 in
Vernon, to $10,000 in Houston. While only six claimed bands
wholly supported by city funds, all but nine sponsored open
air concerts; some of these were financed by the Cham-
bers of Commerce, by the American Legion, and by joint effort of the citizens. Some concerts were given by the Army
bands, some by the Junior Rotary and High School bands.
Abilene, with 32 concerts, headed the list in respect to number
given. All towns that had city auditoriums granted them free
for free concerts; others used their high school auditoriums
similarly. Not one town reported a municipal pipe organ, although there was one in San Antonio and Houston had one
under consideration. No municipal opera was reported, although San Antonio was well on the way to such an institution.
Only Fort Worth reported a municipal orchestra. Dallas, El
Paso, Ennis, Houston and Victoria encouraged community
singing. The smallest amount reported spent on music in the

---

*Abilene, Amarillo, Austin, Beaumont, Belton Brownwood, Burk-
burnett, Childress, Dallas, Denison, Denton, El Paso, Ennis, Fort
Worth, Gainesville, Galveston, Greenville, Hillsboro, Houston, Min-
eral Wells, Navasota, Paris, Ranger, San Angelo, San Marcos, Taylor,
Texarkana, Tyler, Vernon, Victoria, Weatherford and Wichita Falls.

schools was $300 at Denison; this was, no doubt, supplemented by school funds. Outstanding in encouragement of music in the schools were Beaumont, which spent $52,600, and Dallas, whose expenditure was over $98,000. Fifteen of these towns reported music supervisors. Childress was alone in having "no public school music taught."

A survey of the status of community music in the smaller towns that same year showed they were making substantial progress. 63 places reported 18 bands; 56 towns reported 76 orchestras; 54 supported 75 choral organizations; 32 held community sings; and 31 sponsored music memory contests. Among the larger works performed in the smaller towns (San Antonio, Houston, Dallas, Fort Worth, Austin and Waco were excluded from consideration) were: Sullivan's *Pinafore*, Cowen's *Rose Maiden*, Gaul's *Ruth* and *Joan of Arc*, Dubois' *Seven Last Words*, Stainer's *Crucifixion*, Haydn's *Creation*, Mendelssohn's *Elijah*, Rossini's *Stabat Mater*, Bach's *St. Matthew's Passion*, Handel's *Messiah*, Verdi's *Il Trovatore* and *Aïda*, and Gounod's *Faust*.

Other agencies which have promoted music in the various communities have been the libraries and extension departments. Until 1915 very few libraries in the state could boast of any music collection worthy of the name. Between 1915 and 1920 the Dallas Public Library and the Carnegie Library in San Antonio made some real beginnings; the University of Texas accumulated a good working collection for the students; and the smaller educational institutions of the state purchased books on music suited to the various courses taught. The Extension Loan Library, a branch of the Extension Division of the University of Texas, began to assemble clippings, pamphlets, and books to be lent to clubs and individuals over the state. The Visual Instruction Division added a collection of phonograph records to be lent to schools and individuals for short periods.

Publications have also served to promote professional progress and to unite those of common musical interests. Most important as chronicler of musical activities in Texas have been the *Musicale*, later the *Southwestern Musicale;* its successor the *Southwestern Musician;* and the *Music News*. The first of these, a monthly, established in April, 1915, by A. L. Harper, served as an organ of the State Music Teachers Association, the State Federation of Music Clubs; and the Music Merchants Association. On its pages are recorded the activities of music studios and concert halls from 1915 to 1933. After the death of Mr. Harper on April 4, 1931, its management was taken over by others more commercially minded; with the result that its value both as a news organ and as a professional journal declined. It ceased publication with the second issue of volume nineteen.

Even earlier the State Federation of Music Clubs, in an effort to put a copy of its organ in the hands of each member of every federated club, began the publication of the *Music News* with four or five issues a year. It has survived periods of suspension and numerous changes of format.

Although the withdrawal of the clubs support seriously weakened the *Musicale,* its place was taken in 1934 by the *Southwestern Musician* under the general direction of Clyde J. Garrett of Fort Worth. With June, 1936, it had reached the ninth issue of volume two.

The larger dailies of the state have devoted special pages of their Sunday editions to matters of musical interest.

The greatest disseminating agencies of music itself, throughout Texas as throughout the world, are the sound-reproducing machines and the radio, which have brought the best in music within the reach of the poorest home. Before the advent of the broadcasting era, the phonograph of one type or another had entered almost every home and school. Recording was improved until about 1924 whole operas were available on records. Excellent recordings of the best of choral works and symphony made possible instruction in the schools of a type of music hitherto unknown. But barely was the appreciation work well underway in the schools when radio broadcasting began. From the miscellaneous programs at first sent out, the amount of both good and bad music increased amazingly. From the time of the establishment of the two national broadcasting chains, music of the best type was available on some of the programs. Opera over radio from the Chicago and the Metropolitan Opera House, at first only one act and later the whole performance; symphony by Detroit, Minneapolis, Cleveland, Boston and New York Philharmonic orchestras; and vocal and instrumental solos and ensembles by lead-

ing artists were all brought to the home by the magic spark.
In 1922 the *Dallas News* established the first of the larger
broadcasting stations in Texas, WFAA, which now broad-
casts the concerts of the Dallas Symphony and some other
local music of the better type, with a great deal that, from an
educational standpoint, might be better dispensed with. But
since it is sometimes better to have a boy reading a poor book
than no book at all, as he is at least kept out of other mischief,
perhaps it is better for the masses to listen to music of an in-
ferior type and perhaps have their taste slowly cultivated,
than not to listen to music at all. At any rate the phonograph
and the radio have revolutionized music dissemination and
instruction; they have done even more than the printing press
did for literature, because it is possible to enjoy music through
these means without even having to learn to read.

BOOK IV

THE BEGINNINGS OF
CREATIVE WORK

CHAPTER XVII

Texts Folk Music

AS in Europe and other parts of the United States, it was necessary for their musical inheritance to be fully absorbed by the people of Texas before the creative spirit could manifest itself. Not until the years following the Civil War—a period of great spiritual as well as economic upheaval—do we catch the first glimpses of such activity. It is true there were earlier composers of music in Texas, but they followed the models of Europe, Mexico, or the Eastern seaboard. They were musically cultured people; their tendency was to follow existent models to such an extent that little originality was manifested. As in Europe in the Middle Ages, it was from the illiterate or working classes in Texas that more or less original music was to come.

The first native products which showed traces of originality were the songs of the negro, who seemed to absorb music from the composite society about him and then to reflect it in a style distinctly his own. In his music, as in that denominated "creole," are the Spanish rhythms, the strong syncopations, and frequently traces of the Moorish cadences. Its general character is religious; and yet it is colored strangely by human relationships and feelings. The language is figurative; the negro was able to combine his ideas in most unusual ways. The fact that none of his songs were written left more room for the creative impulse; new versions, both of texts and music, were constantly in the making. Most common were the shouting songs; of a more finished type are the spirituals, which breathe on the whole a tone of intense piety and faith. While but few of these have been transcribed, the material for serious study awaits another Dvořák to give to it permanency and form. Other songs of the negro are the work songs; these are largely connected with rural life—especially with corn, cane and cotton field.*

---

*"Seek and Ye Shall Find" and the "Boll Weevil Song" in the Centennial Edition of the *Music Hour* are good examples of these types.

THE YELLOW ROSE OF TEXAS

There's a yel-low rose in Texas that I am going to see, No other darkey knows her, no darkey only me; She cried so when I left her, it like to broke my heart, And if I e-ver find her we never more will part.

CHORUS.

She's the sweetest rose of color this dar-key e-ver knew, Her

She's the sweetest rose of color this dar-key e-ver knew, Her

(128)

FIG. 38

From the city we have the call of the water boy, the hod carrier, the ditch digger. From the convict camp have come many of the work songs, sung perhaps in former happier days in the fields and later adapted to the rock pile or the lumber camp.

(129)

Nor should the love songs of the negro be entirely overlooked although these are less characteristic of the race. In this connection it is of interest that the first song to achieve lasting popularity in which the word "Texas" appeared in the title— "The Yellow Rose of Texas"—was an imitation of just such a song (see pages 128-129).

"Down on de Rollin' Brazos" is another imitation of a negro song associated in the public mind with Texas (see pages 132-133).

While the evolution of negro music in Texas was not radically different from that in other portions of the South, another class gave rise to a specific type, not limited to Texas but which probably had its origin in that state and is certainly most closely associated with it. This is the music of the cowboys. Following the Civil War only one source of income presented itself to the poverty-stricken landowners—the cattle that roamed the plains. But there was no market for them in Texas; no railroad linked the Southwest with the cities of the Middle West; it was necessary that the cattle be driven within reach of the buyers. Then began the trail-driving; the opening of routes by which vast herds of cattle could be moved within reach of marketing centers. Those from Texas have been celebrated in song and story; the Shawnee Trail over Red River up through Arkansas: the Chisholm Trail over Red River to Abilene, Kansas; the Fort Griffin Trail to Dodge City, and the Goodnight-Loving Trail to New Mexico. Over these, vast herds moved northward.

The life of the cowboy was essentially a life in the open. He practiced few of the amenities of polite society, but he knew the vast open spaces. The stars in the sky were close to him; and he shared to some extent the Indian's instinctive feeling of awe and respect toward the creator of all he saw about him. His life was hard; his bed was often the ground; and his "grub" offered little in the way of culinary dainties. Instead, coarse bread, beans, and plenty of meat constituted the daily diet. He was up early; exposed to the extremes of the Texas norther and the blistering suns of summer, he rode his horse long hours without feeling fatigue; he kept watch over the herd through the night. He was employed all the year on the extensive ranches of southwest Texas. The high spots of ranch life were the semi-annual roundups—one in the spring for the purpose of branding the calves and strays; and one in the fall for the selection of beef for the market. In both cases, cattle were gathered from far and wide; and large numbers were put through the branding process or were weeded out as unfit. Following the fall roundup came the slow trail-driving northward.

Separated from society in general as the cowboys were, they evolved forms of expression of their own, and music was one of the channels that expression took. The origin of the cowboy music has been a topic for much discussion. Some believe the cowboy composed his own songs; but those who have studied the subject more closely admit that most of the songs of the cowboy can be traced to old ballads or songs current in that day among more cultured people. Once heard and absorbed by the cowboy, these songs underwent a gradual transformation until the version in which they appeared some decades later is so different from the original as to furnish some justification for those who attribute original composition to the cowboys. In the main, however, the cowboys, like the negroes, were creative only to the extent that they absorbed one type of music so completely that before it became associated in the public mind with them, it had been completely recolored. A comparison of one version of such a song as "Bury Me Not on the Lone Prairie,"* popular in the eighties, with the text and music of "Bury Me Not in the Deep, Deep Sea," issued in 1850, is sufficient to convince even the most skeptical that the cowboy song is fundamentally a paraphrase.

Of these songs there are various types. There is the song he sang while in the saddle, a rhythmical swinging tune, often set to words associated with cattle. Such is "Whoopee-tee-yi-yo."* There is the herding song, sung to lull the cattle at night. There is the camp-fire song, used purely for his own entertainment; its text is frequently quite unprintable. In a study of the rhythms of these songs, Newton Gaines, a grandson

---

*These songs are included in the Centennial Edition of the *Music Hour*.

The cowboy songs are not reproduced in this volume as they are readily available in John A. Lomax's *Cowboy Songs* published by Macmillan; in the cheap version *Songs Texas Sings*, and separately in the artistic settings of Oscar Fox and David Guion.

DOWN ON DE ROLLIN' BRAZOS

FIG. 39

of one of the Tompkins group who came concertizing to Texas in 1850 and settled in San Antonio, says:

The most outstanding quality of these songs, to me, is the rhythm. This rhythm is almost always that of the Western horse; I have discovered and am able to distinguish three different rhythms and only three—the three gaits of the overwhelming majority of our Texas horses, the walk, the trot and the lope. . . .

It is true that the music of the cowboy can usually be traced by

(133)

the expert musician to some popular song of the 70s and 80s or to some Irish or English broadside. . . . Yet in almost every case, one finds that the cowboys have altered the rhythm and melody to suit their pioneer experiences and feelings, of which the song is the expression. . . .There are some melodies among the cowboy songs, however, that I believe have sprung direct from our Western soil. For instance, I think that the tune of the familiar "Bury Me Not on the Lone Prairie". . . . is imitative of the night noises of the prairie, the yelp of the coyote bearing the burden.
A second characteristic is its freeness of expression...
The cowboy, regardless of calendar age, was a boy at heart. He was interested in his own experiences, actual and imaginary; and so a third characteristic of most of his songs is a persistent use of the first person ["they" being generally replaced by "we"]. . . . .
A fifth characteristic of cowboy songs is a spirit of democracy.*

Interesting as these suggestions are, the writer ventures the assertion that careful study of these songs and comparison of them with their originals will not bear out the theories advanced. As an example of the lengths to which imagination and folk-lore can go, take the *Song of the Texas Ranger* beginning "Mount, Mount and Away," which has been credited with the rhythm of the lope, the spirit of the range, and other characteristics of the free life of the prairies. When, however, its original is shown to be "I'm Afloat, I'm afloat on the Wide Rolling Tide" (see pages 46-47), of which the melody is identical and the text a close paraphrase, the rhythm of the saddle is forced to give way to the roll of the waves, not generally credited with being one and the same. Multiplication of such examples is not difficult.

The Texas cowboy is not, historically, an original figure; the Mexican *vaquero*, his prototype, figures in 16th century annals. He appears late in Texas because the presence of hostile Indians deterred him. In the latter part of the 17th century he roamed the El Paso region; in the 18th, he invaded the lower Nueces and the Rio Grande Valley. Separated in turn from his prototype, the Spanish or Indian herdsman, by a much greater period of time, the songs of the Mexican *vaquero* are probably more original than those of the Anglo-American cowboy. Emanating from the high tablelands about the capital, these songs traveled up through Central Mexico; others came along the West Coast and then through Sinaloa

---

Proceedings Texas Folk Lore Society, VII, 145-154.

PALOMITA

Arranged by Manuel Ponce

Traditional Melody

FIG. 40

A Song of the Texas border.

(135)

and Sonora.   A few of these current in the 20th century among all classes of the "frontera" of Texas have been transcribed and aranged in more or less artistic form. Of the more finished versions are those of Manuel Ponce and Ramón Campos. Of these *Palomita* is a good example.

In the field of Mexican cowboy music, little has as yet been done, but its vistas are fascinating to the serious student equipped with the necessary historical, musical and linguistic background.

Under folk music should be included such local adaptations of older songs as linked them with Texas places or events. Into this class fall especially a group of songs connected with the various rivers. Among these are "Down on de Rollin' Brazos," "Can I Forget that Night in June upon the Brazos River," an adaptation from "The Danube;" "Red River Valley," a version of the "Bright Mohawk Valley" and "On Red River Shore"; "On the Banks of the San Antonio," adapted from "Old Salt River"; and various local shifts in the text of "On the Banks of the Blue Moselle." Many of the cowboy songs introduced the Rio Grande in one form or another. Adaptation of other well known songs with an historical setting was also general. "Bruce's Address" by Robert Burns served as the basis for three Texas songs between 1836 and 1846;* "Hohenlinden" by Campbell for others. A detailed study of such adaptations would yield a volume illustrative of the dissemination of various types of music among the people of Texas.

*For titles see pages 26 and 45.

CHAPTER XVIII

Music Composed in Texas or by Texans

THE "Brazos Boat Song," composed in 1831 on the banks of that river by Mary Holley, a cousin of Stephen F. Austin, is the first musical composition written on Texas soil, so far as known to the writer. In the next decade a few composers of varying qualifications made their homes in Texas: Adolf Fuchs, whose existing manuscript volume is representive of his songs; Allyre Bureau, who worked at "La Reunion" in the late fifties; Gustave Fitze at New Waverley, whose music was published by Ditson; and F. W. Smith, professor of music at Baylor College before it was moved from old Independence, composed music of interest in its day. We have mentioned the "Texan youth" who composed music during the Mexican War, and the *March* by Clarence Wharton published during the Civil War. T. B. Bishop in Galveston and Professor Bauer in Dallas, who composed a Christmas Anthem, also deserve mention. The publishing house of Thomas Goggan and Brothers, established in 1866, issued many other works of an ephemeral character written by Texans.

Franz Van der Stucken has already been referred to as the first composer born within the confines of the state to achieve international fame. His work was, however, in no way associated with the state. The first native composer to achieve fame through the use of Texas background was Oscar Fox (1879-   ), who no doubt inherited from his grandfather, Adolf Fuchs, some of his musical ability. Educated in San Antonio and later at Zurich, he served for years as organist, choirmaster and teacher in various Texas cities before achieving fame through his settings of the cowboy songs collected by John Lomax. Only after these paved the way was the merit of his original work recognized. Since 1922 he has labored persistently. "White in the Moon the Long Road Lies," "The Hills of Home" and "The Rain and the River" are among his best known songs. *Corn Silks and Cotton Blossoms* is published here for the first time.

CORN SILKS AND COTTON BLOSSOMS

Whitney Montgomery

Oscar Fox

Corn silks and cotton blossoms,
  Flow'r of the South,—
Thirty years I've tended them
  Thru rain and drouth.
Thirty years I've tended them
  A-toiling hard and long
Dreaming now and then a dream
  That turned into song.

Here I bind them in a wreath
For all the world to see,
Corn silks and cotton blossoms,
And the heart of me.
Corn silks and cotton blossoms,
And the heart of me.

A hitherto unpublished song by Texas' best known song writer.
Used by permission.

(139)

The second native composer to achieve fame is David Guion, born at Ballinger in 1895. He, too, has used as thematic material cowboy and negro melodies; especially has he turned his attention to the humble strata of society, as is shown in his collection of "Alley Tunes." One of these, "The Harmonica Player," and his arrangement of "Turkey in the Straw" are among the best of his instrumental productions; his setting of "Home on the Range" is unquestionably superior; and both the negro and the Indian have received sympathetic treatment by him. Again, it seems that local material has furnished this Texas composer his best subject matter.

In the creation of music in larger forms, the first Texan to achieve fame is Harold Morris, born in San Antonio. After securing his degree at the University of Texas, he studied at the Cincinnati Conservatory of Music. His violin sonata, still unpublished, a Symphonic Poem for orchestra and his piano Concerto have won the praise of outstanding critics. His "Doll's Ballet" is within the range of the average player; but the "Sonata in B-flat Minor" and the "Scherzo" call for more finished technique.

Among song writers, Texas can claim several who have done creditable work: "Wash Day," "Plantation Ditty," "Boats of Mine," and "Parting at Morn" are among the best known of the published works of Anna Stratton (Mrs. Thomas Holden) who was born in Cleburne and educated at the University of Texas. Kathleen Blair Clark, while a composition student of Arthur Claasen, produced a few songs which showed promise—among them "Fanchonette" and "Little Rose of May." Horace Clark, born in Houston, the son of a professor at old Baylor College, received his early training under Mrs. Grünewald, the grandmother of Olga Samaroff. Although he attended the New England Conservatory, it is the coloring of the South that pervades his work. "Songs from the South," one of his best known groups, includes those of the negro, such as "Aunt Sally," "Over Jordan," and "When Old Aunt Lindy Sings." Raide Britain of Amarillo follows the Texas tradition with "Hail Texas" and "A Western Suite" which includes five sketches—"On the Plains," "The Covered Wagon," "Mirage," "Campfire" and "Stampede." Newell Cummins, born in Denison and a student of Edward McDow-

ell, has made some arrangements of cowboy and southern melodies; Annette Myers, born in Marshall and a graduate of the
American Conservatory in Chicago, has written a string quartette, a "Reverie" for cello and piano and a song, "Texas Our
Native State." Alice Mayfield Brooks of San Antonio has used
negro themes in an interesting manner. Louise Daggett Fisher
has written songs and music for strings that show musical insight.

Composers born outside of Texas but who have done work
worthy of attention while residents of the state include: Reuben Davies, born in 1891 and educated at the University of
Kansas and the Institute of Musical Art, whose "Western
Romance," "Echoes from Colorado," "Tishomingo," and "From
a Log Cabin" have a western coloring; Anna E. George, a
native of Mississppi, educated at Bush Conservatory, a few of
whose compositions, such as "The Creek" and "The Prairie
Pictures," possibly have a Texas background; Julius Jahn, of
Dutch-French ancestry educated at Munich and Vienna, who
has written especially for women's voices "Barcarolle," "The
River," "Laughing Song," "Lullaby," "Evening," and "Morning." The most voluminous composer of this group and the
one most closely associated with Texas life is William J. Marsh,
born in England, but a cotton broker in Texas since 1904, and
the composer of the State song, "Texas, Our Texas." As he
has served for years as an organist and choir director, many
of his works are sacred in type—masses, motets, anthems,
Christmas and Easter songs. Local coloring is to be found in
"Chinita"—a Spanish serenade—and "Bluebonnet Time." In
San Antonio one of the outstanding composers is John M.
Steinfeldt, born in Hanover, Germany, but educated mainly
at the Cincinnati Conservatory. He, too, has written much
sacred music, including a "Mass in G Minor." Marked by
Texas coloring are his fine choral *Hymn to Texas* and a piano
number,"At the Mission." His interest lies mainly in the field of
piano music. Both Arthur Claasen and Carl Hahn deserve
mention here, although their best work was done outside of
the state. At Southern Methodist University is Harold Hart
Todd, born in Ohio, and educated at Oberlin and the University of Nebraska, whose principal contribution has been his

editorial work on the Cokesbury Hymnal. At Westmoorland College, San Antonio, is Carl Venth, born in Cologne in 1860 and educated under Hiller and Wieniawski. Once concert master of the Flemish Opera at Brussels, he came to·America in 1880, played in the Metropolitan Orchestra, conducted the Brooklyn Symphony, and was concert master of the St. Paul orchestra. In Texas, he has served as director of the Kidd Key Conservatory, of the Dallas and Fort Worth Symphony, and of the School of Fine Arts at Texas Woman's College. His three one-act operas and a Centennial song, "I am a Texan" are among his Texas productions; his *Pan in America* won the National Federation of Music Clubs prize in 1923, and his numerous cantatas have had wide rendition. His comic opera "Fair Betty" was presented in Fort Worth in 1916. He has a Texas opera ready for presentation in 1936.

★　★　★

The bits of history recalled by these pages can only be fairly interpreted when fitted into the larger picture of American and world culture, of which they form a part. When the first European music was taught in Texas, John Sebastian Bach was not yet born; Spanish music was being sung during the lifetime of Handel, Haydn, Mozart, Beethoven and Schubert; the Republic of Texas came into being on the crest of the Romantic Movement, when Chopin, Mendelssohn and Schumann were mature men; and the Civil War period, represented in Texas by the music of the "Old South" is contemporary with the beginning of the modern school of composers. While distinct types of folk music were evolving in Texas, Russian and Spanish composers were beginning to turn their attention to native themes; Liszt and Brahms made known to the world the variety and richness of Hungarian music; and Dvořák awoke the pride and enthusiasm of the Czechs for their own folk music. Had one sought a century earlier in those countries for the music of the people in printed form, there would have been even less of interest found than is presented here in connection with Texas. What each of these countries has since contributed in the form of modern music is the adaptation and utilization of existent material. Texas and her various

(142)

folk themes still await the composer who is to give them adequate expression in the form of a great suite, choral work, symphony or opera. Perhaps this sketch, pieced together from the insignificant items of past life in Texas, may serve to suggest that goal, or inspire the effort which will create in this state, from themes typically Texan, a musical masterpiece of the first rank.

APPENDIX

TEXAS CONCERT CALENDAR, 1920-1921

AUSTIN

Nov. 5—Josef Lhevinne (Mrs. Katherine Buford Peeples).

ABILENE

Oct. 11—Marie Tiffany (Simmons College).

Oct. 29—Josef Lhevinne (Simmons College).

Jan. ..—Thelma Given (Simmons College).

Paul Althouse and the Victor Orchestra will be presented by the Christian College during the season, but dates have not been assigned.

AMARILLO

Oct. 25—Reed Miller and Nevada Van de Veer (Amarillo College of Music).

Dec. ..—Marie Rappold (Amarillo College of Music).

Feb. 17—Florence Hardeman and Stewart Wille (Amarillo College of Music).

BELTON

Nov. 4—Rafael Diaz and Eddy Brown (Belton Music Club).

Nov. ..—Great Lakes String Quartette (Baylor College).

Dec. 10—Marie Rappold (Belton Music Club).

Dec. ..—Albert Lindquist (Baylor College).

Jan. 25—Redpath Concert Orchestra (Baylor College).

Feb. ..—Mme. Schumann-Heink (Belton Music Club).

March 23—Reinald Warrenrath and E. Robert Schmitz (Belton Music Club).

April ..—Anna Case (Belton Music Club).

CORSICANA

Nov. 2—Bertha Freeman Ashberry (Nevin Club).

Nov. 12—Lambert Murphy (Nevin Club).

DALLAS

(Symphony Orchestra date not assigned.)

Oct. 11—Allen McQuhae (Catholic Ladies' Aid Society).

Oct 28—Zoellner Quartette (University Club).

Nov. 1—Rafael Diaz and Marie Tiffany (E. G. Council).

Nov. 4—Josef Lhevinne (Schubert Choral Club).

Nov. 7—Merle Alcock (Dallas Band).

Nov. 8—Pietro Yon (American Legion).

Nov . 10—Scottish Rite Octette

Nov. 10—Julia Claussen (Musicale Concert Bureau).

Nov. 18—Sophie Braslau (E. D. Behrends).

Nov. 22—Eddy Brown and Reuben Davies (E. G. Council).

Nov. 29—Helen Stanley (Musicale Concert Bureau).

Dec. 2—Mary Garden (Mmes. Mason and MacDonald).

Dec. 5—Freza Green. assisted by Dallas Artist (Dallas Band).

Dec. 13—Marie Rappold (E. G. Council).

Dec. 25—American Opera Company (Dallas Male Chorus).

Jan. 5—Harvard Glee Club (Dallas Male Chorus).

Jan 11—Fritz Kreisler (Mmes. Mason and MacDonald).

Jan 11—Percy Grainger (Musicale Concert Bureau).

Jan 15—Boys' Choir (University Club).

Jan 17—Duncan Dancers and Beryl Rubinetein, pianist (Musicale Concert Bureau).

Jan. 24—Benno Moisewitch (E. D. Behrends).

Jan. 24—Arthur Middleton (E. G. Council).

Jan. 25—Dallas Male Chorus (University Club).

---

*As announced in *The Musicale*, November, 1920.

Jan. 31—Grace Wagner, Caroline Lazzari, Renato Zanelli, Frank LaForge at the piano (Mmes. Mason and MacDonald).

Feb. 3—Mary Jordan (Musicale Concert Bureau).

Feb. 13—Albert Lindquist (Dallas Band).

Feb. —Thurlow Lieurance, Edna Wooley and George Tack(Musicale Concert Bureau).

Feb. 17—Maggie Teyte (Schubert Choral Club).

March 7—American Operatic Company (University Club).

March 7—Mabel Garrison (E. D. Behrends).

March ..—New York Philharmonic Orchestra (Dallas Male Chorus).

March 13—Albert Spalding (Dallas Band).

March 14—Dallas Symphony Orchestra (University Club).

March 17—Harold Bauer (Mmes. Mason and MacDonald).

March 21—The Kennedys (University Club).

March 22—Reinald Werrenrath (Musicale Concert Bureau).

March 28—Vera Poppe (University Club).

March 29—Adolph Bolm Ballet and Little Symphony Orchestra (Musicale Concert Bureau).

April 4—Morgan Kingston (E. G. Council).

April 10—Louis Graveure (Dallas Band).

April 22—Forrest Lamont (E. G. Behrends).

May 8—Gabrielle Besanzoni (Dallas Band).

May ..—Scotti Opera Company Mason and MacDonald).

May ..—Music Week: Annual meetings of the Texas Teachers' Association, Texas Federation of Music Clubs and Texas Music Merchants' Association.

FORT WORTH

Oct. 14—Allen McQuhae (American Legion).

Oct. 19—Caruso (Harmony Club).

Oct. 28—Josef Lhevinne (Inez Hudgins).

Nov. 3—Merle Alcock (Euterpean Club).

Nov. 12—Julia Claussen (American Legion).

Nov. 15—Lambert Murphy (Euterpean Club).

Nov. 17—May Peterson (American Legion).

Nov. 30—Helen Stanley (Inez Hudgins).

Dec. 3—Mary Garden (Harmony Club).

Jan. 10—Percy Grainger (Harmony Club)

Jan. 16—Thelma Given(Inez Hudgins).

Jan. 26—Mary Jordan (Inez Hudgins).

Jan. ..—Louis Graveure (American Legion).

Feb. 15—Thurlow Lieurance; Edna Wooley, soprano; George Tack, flutist (Inez Hudgins).

March 14—E. Robert Schmitz and Olive Kline (Euterpean Club).

Week of March 27—Anna Case (Harmony Club).

March ...—Forrest Lamont (American Legion).

After Easter—LeDesca Loveland and Edgar Schofield (Inez Hudgins).

April 15—New York Philharmonic Orchestra (Harmony Club).

HOUSTON

Oct. 22—Enrico Caruso (Edna W. Saunders).

Nov. 15-17—San Carlo Opera Company (Edna W. Saunders).

Nov. 23—Sophie Braslau (Edna W. Saunders).

March ..—Chicago Grand Opera Company, two performances (Edna W. Saunders).

April 12—New York Philharmonic Orchestra, matinee and night (Edna W. Saunders).

May 8-10—Scotti Grand Opera Company (Edna W. Saunders).

Appendix

RUSK
Oct. 22—Merle Alcock (Rusk College Conservatory).
Feb. 21—Yolando Mero (Rusk College Conservatory).
March 22—Olive Kline (Rusk College Conservatory).

SAN ANGELO
Jan. 28—Renato Zanelli and Frank LaForge (J. Culberson Deal).
Feb. 25—Eight Victor Artists (J. Culberson Deal).
March 4—Mme. Frances Alda (J. Culberson Deal).

SAN ANTONIO
Oct. 12—Rafael Diaz (San Antonio Symphony Society).
Nov. 5—Josef Lhevine (Tuesday Musicale Club and Chaminade Society).
Nov. ..—San Carlo Opera Company (Tuesday Musicale Club and Chaminade Society).
Nov. 16—Julia Claussen (Alva Wilgus). Thelma Given and Genia Zielinska, joint recital (Alva Wilgus).
Nov. 22—Sophie Braslau (Mozart Society).
Dec. 6—Helen Stanley (Mozart Society).
March 19—Giovanni Martinelli (Mozart Society).
March 1—Paul Althouse (Alva Wilgus).
April ..—LeDesca Loveland and Edgar Schofield, joint recital (Alva Wilgus).

SHERMAN
Oct. 5—Bomar Cramer (Kidd-Key Music Club).
Oct. 15—Anna Case (Austin College).

Oct. 28—Frank Renard (Kidd-Key Conservatory).
Oct 29—Marie Tiffany (George Condon).
Nov. 5—Eddy Brown (Kidd-Key Music Club).
Nov. 14—Julia Claussen (Kidd-Key Music Club).
Nov. 19—Marie Rappold (Austin College).
Dec. 2—Henrica Jones (Kidd-Key Conservatory).
Jan. 14—Percy Grainger (Kidd-Key Musical Club).
Feb. 11—Maggie Teyte (Kidd-Key Music Club).
March 14—Albert Spalding (George Congdon).
March 14—Paul Althouse (Kidd-Key Music Club).
March 15—Harold Bauer (Kidd-Key Music Club).
Mr. Hans Richard, Miss Ethel Rader and Mr. Harold Loring, lecture-recital, will be presented on dates to be determined.

TEXARKANA
Nov. 9—Merle Alcock (Mrs. Ray Eberson).
Jan. 27.—Salvatore de Stefano and Mrs. Eberson, joint recital (Mrs. Ray Eberson).
May 3—Allen McQuhae (Mrs. Ray Eberson).

WACO
Nov. 2-5—San Carlo Grand Opera Company (Cotton Palace Exposition).

WICHITA FALLS
Nov. 29—Marie Rappold (Musician's Club).
March 28—Morgan Kingston (Musicians' Club).

INDEX

Index

College of Industrial Arts, see
Texas State College for Women
College entrance credit in music,
113
Colleges, 60, 91
"*Columbia, land of liberty,*" 32
Columbus, 95
"*Come dwell with me,*" 27
"*Come, flowers to me,*" 57
"*Come, oh come with me.*" 59-60
Comfort, 96, 97
Community music, 89, 120-122
Composers, 26, 35-6, 38, 41, 77, 137
Compositions, musical, 78, 104,
127, 137-143; instruction in, 82
Concert managers, 77, 144-146
Concerts in Texas, 17, 28, 29, 34,
37, 41, 62, 63, 69-78, 92, 101, 104,
108-111, 120, 121
Concert halls, 28, 41, 76, 105
Concordia (New Braunfels), 96
Concordia Club (Dallas), 79
"Confederate Flag", 61
"Confederate Grand March", 62
Cornet, 78
Considerant, Victor, 55, 58
Conservatory of music, 70, 77
Contests, 116
Corpus Christi, 45
Corri, Henry, 28
Corsicana, 111
Cosmopolites, 79
Cowboy songs, 37, 65, 66, 130-137
140, 141
Creation, 76, 122
Creole music, 53, 127
Crooker, Fanny L., 75-76, 98
Crucifixion, 122
Culture, 3
Cummins, Newell, 140
Curricula, music, 114-118
Czar und Zimmerman, 105
Czechs in Texas, 26, 58, 60
Cymbals, 26

Dallas, French in, 55-58
Dallas, music in, 76, 77-79, 92, 97,
98, 104, 106, 107, 114, 120-122
124, 137; Glee Club, 78; Sym-
phony Orchestra, 109, 110
Daly, Abel, 77
Damrosch, Leopold, 37
Dance halls, 41
Dances, 4, 5, 9, 12, 14, 17, 27, 29,
53, 74

Dancing teachers, 78
Daughter of St. Mark, 101
Davies, Reuben, 141
Davis, Mollie Moore, 63, 104
"Days of Absence,', 26
"Dead at Buena Vista," 50
Dean, W. K., 49
De Bar, Mrs., 28
Debussy, C., 110
De Falla, M., 110
"De larga jornada," 18
Delgado, Eusebio, 71
Denison, 121, 122, 140
Denton, 113, 121
Denver, 111
Derthick music clubs, 119
Detroit Symphony Orchestra, 111
Deutsche Lied, Das," 97
Deutsche Schriften in Texas, 37
Devine, Judge T. J., 75
Diaz, Rafaelo, 106
Diehl, Anton, 98
Ditson Co., Oliver, 41, 71, 137
"Dixie," 83
"Dixie War Song," 61
"Does your Mother Know," 27
"Doll's Ballet," 140
Domenech, Emanuel, 55
Don Giovanni, 104
Doran, John, 32
Douai, Adolf, 37, 94
Double bass, 108
"Down on de rollin' Brazos," 132-
33
Dramatic performances, 20, 76
Drummer, 26
"Drummer Boy of Shiloh," 63
Drums, 25
Dubina, 58
Dubois, Theodore, 122
Dunn, George, 63
Dunn, John G., 50
Durivage, F. A., 48
Durriage, T. A., 45
Duvernoy, Gustave, 82
"Dying Camille," 65

Eaton, E. O., 65
Eberhardt, Louis, 75
Eckert, Carl A. F., 97
Eckhardt, Profesor, 70,
Edison, Thomas, 84
Education, musical, 62, 69, 70, 74-
77, 80-85, 113-118; physical, 74;
State Department of, 114-118;

(149)

Index

Index

Index